ISBN 0-8373-6632-1

DANTES–32

Rudman's Question and Answers on the

DANTES SUBJECT STANDARDIZED TESTS

Subject Examination In...

PRINCIPLES OF ECONOMICS

Questions and Answers

NLC

NATIONAL LEARNING CORPORATION

212 MICHAEL DRIVE, SYOSSET, NEW YORK 11791 (516) 921-8888

National Learning Corporation

212 Michael Drive, Syosset, New York 11791

(516) 921-8888

PRINTED IN THE UNITED STATES OF AMERICA

PASSBOOK®

NOTICE

This book is *SOLELY* intended for, is sold *ONLY* to, and its use is *RESTRICTED* to *individual*, bona fide applicants or candidates who qualify by virtue of having seriously filed applications for appropriate license, certificate, professional and/or promotional advancement, higher school matriculation, scholarship, or other legitimate requirements of educational and/or governmental authorities.

This book is *NOT* intended for use, class instruction, tutoring, training, duplication, copying, reprinting, excerption, or adaptation, etc., by:

(1) Other Publishers
(2) Proprietors and/or Instructors of "Coaching" and/or Preparatory Courses
(3) Personnel and/or Training Divisions of commercial, industrial, and governmental organizations
(4) Schools, colleges, or universities and/or their departments and staffs, including teachers and other personnel
(5) Testing Agencies or Bureaus
(6) Study groups which seek by the purchase of a single volume to copy and/or duplicate and/or adapt this material for use by the group as a whole without having purchased individual volumes for each of the members of the group
(7) Et al.

Such persons would be in violation of appropriate Federal and State statutes.

PROVISION OF LICENSING AGREEMENTS. — Recognized educational commercial, industrial, and governmental institutions and organizations, and others legitimately engaged in educational pursuits, including training, testing, and measurement activities, may address a request for a licensing agreement to the copyright owners, who will determine whether, and under what conditions, including fees and charges, the materials in this book may be used by them. In other words, a licensing facility *exists* for the legitimate use of the material in this book on other than an individual basis. However, it is asseverated and affirmed here that the materials in this book *CANNOT* be used without the receipt of the express permission of such a licensing agreement from the Publishers.

NATIONAL LEARNING CORPORATION
212 Michael Drive
Syosset, New York 11791

Inquiries re licensing agreements should be addressed to:
The President
National Learning Corporation
212 Michael Drive
Syosset, New York 11791

PASSBOOK SERIES®

THE *PASSBOOK SERIES®* has been created to prepare applicants and candidates for the ultimate academic battlefield—the examination room.

At some time in our lives, each and every one of us may be required to take an examination—for validation, matriculation, admission, qualification, registration, certification, or licensure.

Based on the assumption that every applicant or candidate has met the basic formal educational standards, has taken the required number of courses, and read the necessary texts, the *PASSBOOK SERIES®* furnishes the one special preparation which may assure passing with confidence, instead of failing with insecurity. Examination questions—together with answers—are furnished as the basic vehicle for study so that the mysteries of the examination and its compounding difficulties may be eliminated or diminished by a sure method.

This book is meant to help you pass your examination provided that you qualify and are serious in your objective.

The entire field is reviewed through the huge store of content information which is succinctly presented through a provocative and challenging approach—the question-and-answer method.

A climate of success is established by furnishing the correct answers at the end of each test.

You soon learn to recognize types of questions, forms of questions, and patterns of questioning. You may even begin to anticipate expected outcomes.

You perceive that many questions are repeated or adapted so that you gain acute insights, which may enable you to score many sure points.

You learn how to confront new questions, or types of questions, and to attack them confidently and work out the correct answers.

You note objectives and emphases, and recognize pitfalls and dangers, so that you may make positive educational adjustments.

Moreover, you are kept fully informed in relation to new concepts, methods, practices, and directions in the field.

You discover that you are actually taking the examination all the time: you are preparing for the examination by "taking" an examination, not by reading extraneous and/or supererogatory textbooks.

In short, this PASSBOOK®, used directedly, should be an important factor in helping you to pass your test.

DANTES Subject Standardized Tests

INTRODUCTION

The DANTES (Defense Activity for Non-Traditional Education Support) subject standardized tests are comprehensive college and graduate level examinations given by the Armed Forces, colleges and graduate schools as end-of-subject course evaluation final examinations or to obtain college equivalency credits in the various subject areas tested.

Active military personnel may take CLEP (College-Level Examination Program) examinations without charge through the DANTES program. Information about DANTES and CLEP may be obtained from the Test Control Officers at military installations, and from Educational Testing Service in Princeton, New Jersey.

The DANTES Examination Program enables students to obtain college credit for what they have learned on the job, through self-study, personal interest, correspondence courses or by any other means. It is used by colleges and universities to award college credit to students who demonstrate that they know as much as students completing an equivalent college course. It is a cost-efficient, time-saving way for students to use their knowledge to accomplish their educational goals.

Most schools accept the American Council on Education (ACE) recommendations for the minimum score required and the amount of credit awarded, but not all schools do. Be sure to check the policy regarding the score level required for credit and the number of credits to be awarded.

Not all tests are accepted by all institutions. Even when a test is accepted by an institution, it may not be acceptable for every program at that institution. Before considering testing, ascertain the acceptability of a specific test for a particular course.

Colleges and universities that administer DANTES tests may administer them to any applicant -- or they may administer the tests only to students registered at their institution. Decisions about who will be allowed to test are made by the school. Students should contact the test center to determine current policies and schedules for DANTES testing.

Colleges and universities authorized to administer DANTES tests usually do so throughout the calendar year. Each school sets its own fee for test administration and establishes its own testing schedule. Contact the representative at the administering school directly to make arrangements for testing.

Your Experience Can Earn You Credit.

It's a fact. People learn in many ways . . . through hobbies . . . interests . . . reading . . . work. The DANTES Program is a way for you to "cash in" on what you've learned from *your* experiences.

Take advantage of DANTES tests to earn college credit for what you know. More than 30 subjects are offered. There are bound to be areas where your knowledge can pay off academically.

Here are just a few of the program's benefits for you:

- ***Time and Money Saver***
  You don't have to sit through classes and pay for courses when you already know most of what's being taught and can learn the rest yourself.
- ***Credits Widely Accepted***
  Hundreds of colleges nationwide now give credit for DANTES tests. And the list is growing!
- ***Quicker Route to the Degree***
  Your dreams are a little closer than you thought possible. With DANTES.
- ***Start Fast***
  No need to wait to take advanced courses. Passing DANTES tests gives you a real head start.

Sound Good? Here's How to Get Going!

Check with your college to see if it administers the DANTES program. If the college doesn't but would like to, ask that someone **call collect** (609-951-1756) or write to the DANTES Program Office (see address below).

If you find that your college *accepts* DANTES credits, but does not *administer* the tests, here's what you do —

- Write to the DANTES Program Office for a list of colleges that administer the test. Chances are there's one nearby.
- Call any of the ETS Regional Offices (Tucker, GA; Oakland, CA; Evanston, IL; Phoenix, AZ; and Princeton, NJ. DANTES tests are given at all of those locations.
- In the military or in the reserves? DoD employees and family members may be able to take DANTES tests at a Military Education Office or Navy Campus Office.

Check Out the DANTES Test List.

Match the titles with the things you have learned. Consider how much college credit you might gain by taking some DANTES tests.

Your college should have fact sheets with more information about each DANTES test. If not, please write to us directly, or e-mail us at dantes@chauncey.com. Tell us which subjects interest you.

DANTES Program Office
Educational Testing Service
Princeton, NJ 08541-0001

MATHEMATICS

Introductory College Algebra
- Functions and graphs
- Fundamental algebraic operations
- Linear equations, inequalities, word problems
- Radicals and exponents

Principles of Statistics
- Descriptive statistics
- Correlation, regression, probability
- Chance models, sampling, test of significance

SOCIAL SCIENCE

Art of the Western World
- Greece and Rome
- Romanesque and Gothic
- Renaissance
- Baroque, rococo, neoclassicism, romanticism
- Twentieth century

The Civil War and Reconstruction
- Causes of the war
- Political situations and the war between 1861 and 1865
- Reconstruction

Contemporary Western Europe
- Historical background
- Political systems
- Societal issues
- Integration

Criminal Justice
- Criminal behavior
- Police and criminal justice system
- Court system
- Corrections

Drug and Alcohol Abuse
- Pharmacological principles
- Classification of drugs
- Properties of alcohol, sedative hypnotics, narcotic analgesics, stimulants, hallucinogens and other drugs
- Prevention/treatment

Foundations of Education
- Contemporary issues in education
- Past and current influences on education
- Interrelationships between contemporary issues and influences, past or current, in education

Fundamentals of Counseling
- Counselor roles and functions
- Counseling relationships
- Theoretical approaches
- Social and cultural foundations

General Anthropology
- Anthropology branches, methodologies, and theoretical perspectives
- Physical anthropology and archeology
- Nature of culture
- Social, economic, political, and religious organization

A History of the Vietnam War
- The first Vietnam War (1945-1954)
- LBJ goes to war (1964-1965)
- Tet Offensive (1968)
- Vietnamizing the war (1968-1973)
- Peace is at hand (1968-1973)

Human/Cultural Geography
- Basic facts and concepts
- Culture and environment
- Spatial processes
- Regional geography

Introduction to Law Enforcement
- U.S. criminal justice and police systems
- Issues and organization of police
- Constitutional law and precedents

Introduction to the Modern Middle East
- Geography and early history
- Nineteenth and early twentieth century
- First and Second World wars
- Soviet-U.S. rivalry, Suez Crisis, Iranian Revolution, Persian Gulf Crisis

Lifespan Developmental Psychology
- Biological development
- Perception, learning, and memory
- Social, emotional, and personality development
- Cognition and language

BUSINESS

Business Law II
- Sales of goods
- Debtor and creditor relations
- Business organizations
- Property
- Commercial paper

Business Mathematics
- Basic computation — fractions, percents, ratios, graphs
- Business applications

Introduction to Business
- Economic, international, government, and ownership issues
- Management process
- Human resources and production
- Marketing, finance

Introduction to Computers with Programming in BASIC
- Hardware, software, data management
- Communications and connectivity
- BASIC: I/O, expressions, loops, conditionals, strings, arrays

Management Information Systems
- Systems theory, analysis and design of systems
- Hardware and software
- Database management
- Telecommunications
- Management of the MIS functional area, informational support

Money and Banking
- Role of commercial banks and other intermediaries
- Federal Reserve System
- Macroeconomic activity, U.S. policy, international system

Personal Finance
- Financial goals, budgeting, cash management, economic terminology
- Credit, debt, and major purchases
- Taxes and insurance
- Investments, retirement and estate planning

Personnel/Human Resource Management
- Employment actions
- Training and development
- Performance appraisals
- Compensation and personnel legislation
- Labor relations

Principles of Finance
- Financial statements and ratio analysis
- Capital budgeting
- Time value of money
- Break-even and leverage, common stock

Principles of Financial Accounting
- General concepts and principles
- Financial statements
- Accruals and deferrals
- Current accounts

Principles of Supervision
- Roles and responsibilities
- Management functions
- Legal issues, stress management, unions, productivity and quality concerns

Organizational Behavior
- Individual and group processes and characteristics
- Organizational processes and behavior
- Change and development processes

APPLIED TECHNOLOGY

Technical Writing
- Elements of technical reports
- Style, grammar, mechanics, organizing
- Types of technical reports

HUMANITIES

Ethics in America
- Ethical traditions
- Analysis of issues in relationships
- Tradition versus analysis of issues

Introduction to World Religions
- Dimensions and approaches
- Primal religions, Hinduism, Buddhism, Confucianism, Taoism, Judaism, Christianity, Islam

Principles of Public Speaking
- Topics and purposes
- Organization and supporting materials
- Language, style, and delivery
- Audience analysis and adaptation

PHYSICAL SCIENCE

Astronomy
- The solar system
- The sun and stars
- Our galaxy and the universe
- Measurement

Environment and Humanity: The Race to Save the Planet
- Ecological concepts
- Human impact on the environment
- Environmental management
- Political processes and the future

Here's to Your Health
- Mental health and behavior
- Human development
- Substance use and abuse
- Fitness and nutrition
- Risk factors and disease
- Consumer awareness, environmental concerns

Physical Geology
- Earth materials
- Surface processes
- Internal earth processes
- Applications

Principles of Physical Science I
- Physics: Newton's laws, energy, thermodynamics optics, electricity, and magnetism
- Chemistry: matter, atomic theory and structure, chemical reactions

NOTE:

MOST SCHOOLS DO NOT ACCEPT ALL TESTS FOR ALL PROGRAMS. CHECK WITH THE SCHOOL FROM WHICH YOU EXPECT TO RECEIVE CREDIT.

ECONOMISTS

NATURE OF THE WORK

Economists study the ways a society uses scarce resources such as land, labor, raw materials, and machinery to produce goods and services. They analyze the costs and benefits of distributing and consuming these goods and services. Their research might focus on topics such as energy costs, electronic components production, farm prices, or imports.

Some economists who are primarily theoreticians may develop theories through the use of mathematical models to explain the causes of business cycles and inflation or the effects of unemployment and tax policy. Most economists, however, are concerned with practical applications of economic policy in a particular area, such as finance, labor, agriculture, transportation, energy, or health. They use their understanding of economic relationships to advise business firms, insurance companies, banks, securities firms, industry associations, labor unions, government agencies, and others.

Depending on the topic under study, economists devise methods and procedures for obtaining data they need. For example, sampling techniques may be used to conduct a survey, and econometric modeling techniques may be used to develop projections. Preparing reports usually is an important part of the economist's job. He or she may be called upon to review and analyze all the relevant data, prepare tables and charts, and write up the results in clear, concise language.

Being able to present economic and statistical concepts in a meaningful way is particularly important for economists whose research is policy directed. Market research analysts who work for business firms may be asked to provide management with information to make decisions on marketing and pricing of company products; to look at the advisability of adding new lines of merchandise, opening new branches, or diversifying the company's operations; to analyze the effect of changes in the tax laws; or to prepare economic and business forecasts. Business economists working for firms that carry on operations abroad may be asked to prepare forecasts of foreign economic conditions.

Economists who work for government agencies assess economic conditions in the United States and abroad and estimate the economic impact of specific changes in legislation or public policy. For example, they may study how changes in the minimum wage affect teenage unemployment. Most government economists are in the fields of agriculture, business, finance, labor, transportation, utilities, urban economics, or international trade. For example, economists in the U.S. Department of Commerce study domestic production, distribution, and consumption of commodities or services; those in the Federal Trade Commission prepare industry analyses to assist in enforcing Federal statutes designed to eliminate unfair, deceptive, or monopolistic practices in interstate commerce; and those in the Bureau of Labor Statistics analyze data on prices, wages, employment, and productivity.

WORKING CONDITIONS

Economists working for government agencies and private firms have structured work schedules. They may work alone writing reports, preparing statistical charts, and using computers and calculators. Or they may be an integral part of a research team. Most work under pressure of deadlines and tight schedules, and sometimes must work overtime. Their routine may be interrupted by special requests for data, letters, meetings, or conferences. Travel may be necessary to collect data or attend conferences.

Economics faculty have flexible work schedules, dividing their time among teaching, research, consulting, and administrative responsibilities.

EMPLOYMENT

Economists hold about 50,000 jobs. Private industry -- particularly economic and market research firms, management consulting firms, advertising firms, banks, and securities, investment, and insurance companies -- employed over two-thirds of all salaried economists. The remainder were employed by a wide range of government agencies, primarily in the Federal Government. The Department of Labor, Agriculture, and State are the largest Federal employers. About 1 out of every 5 economists runs his or her own consulting business. A number of economists combine a full-time job in government or business with part-time or consulting work in another setting.

Employment of economists is concentrated in large cities. The largest numbers are in New York City and Washington, D.C. Some work abroad for companies with major international operations; for the Department of State and other U.S. Government agencies; and for international organizations.

Besides the jobs described above, an estimated 30,000 persons held economics and marketing faculty positions in colleges and universities.

TRAINING, OTHER QUALIFICATIONS, AND ADVANCEMENT

A bachelor's degree with a major in economics or marketing is sufficient for many beginning research, administrative, management trainee, and sales jobs. The undergraduate curriculum includes courses such as microeconomics, macroeconomics, business cycles, economic and business history, economic development of selected areas, money and banking, international economics, public finance, industrial organization, labor economics, comparative economic systems, economics of national planning, urban economic problems, marketing, and consumer behavior analysis. Courses in related disciplines, such as political science, psychology, organizational behavior, socialogy, finance, business law, and international relations, are suggested. Because of the importance of quantitative skills to economists, courses in mathematics, business and economic statistics, sampling theory and survey design, and computer science are highly recommended.

Graduate training increasingly is required for most economist jobs and for advancement to more responsible positions. Areas of specialization at the graduate level include advanced economic theory, mathematical economics, econometrics, history of economic thought, and comparative economic systems and planning. Other areas include economic history, economic development, environmental and natural resource economics, industrial organization, marketing, institutional economics, international economics, labor economics, monetary economics, public finance, regional and urban economics, and social policy. Students should select graduate schools strong in specialties in which they are interested. Some schools help graduate students find internships or part-time employment in government agencies, economic consulting firms, financial institutions, or market research firms. Work experience and contacts can be useful in testing career preferences and learning about the job market for economists.

In the Federal Government, candidates for entrance positions generally need a college degree with a minimum of 21 semester hours of economics and 3 hours of statistics, accounting, or calculus. However, because competition is keen, additional education or experience may be required.

For a job as a college instructor in many junior colleges and small 4-year schools, a master's degree generally is the minimum requirement. In some colleges and universities, however, a Ph.D. and extensive publication are required for a professorship and for tenure, which are increasingly difficult to obtain.

In government, industry, research organizations, and consulting firms, economists who have a graduate degree usually can qualify for more responsible research and administrative positions. A Ph.D. is necessary for top positions in many organizations. Many corporation and government executives have a strong background in economics or marketing.

Over 1,200 colleges and universities offer bachelor's degree programs in economics and marketing; over 600, master's and about 130, doctoral programs.

Persons considering careers as economists should be able to work accurately with detail since much time is spent on data analysis. Patience and persistence are necessary because economists may spend long hours on independent study and problem solving. At the same time, they must be able to work well with others. Economists must be objective and systematic in their work and be able to express themselves effectively both orally and in writing. Creativity and intellectual curiosity are essential for success in this field, just as they are in other areas of scientific endeavor.

JOB OUTLOOK

Employment of economists is expected to grow faster than the average for all occupations through the year 2000. Most job openings, however, will result from the need to replace experienced economists who transfer to other occupations, or retire or leave the labor force for other reasons.

Opportunities should be best in manufacturing, financial services, advertising agencies, research organizations, and consulting firms, reflecting the complexity of the domestic and international economies and increased reliance on quantitative methods of analyzing business trends, forecasting sales, and planning of purchasing and production. The continued need for economic analyses by lawyers, accountants, engineers, health service administrators, urban and regional planners, environmental scientists, and others will also increase the number of jobs for economists. Little or no change is expected in the employment of economists in the Federal Government -- in line with the rate of growth projected for the Federal work force as a whole. Employment of economists in State and local government combined is expected to grow more slowly than the average. While courses in economics are increasingly popular, college enrollments are expected to decline through the year 2000 -- resulting in declining employment in colleges and universities. As a result, some highly qualified economics graduates will enter nonacademic positions.

A strong background in economic theory, statistics, and econometrics provides the tools for acquiring any specialty within the field. Those skilled in quantitative techniques and their application to economic modeling and forecasting and market research, including the use of computers, should have the best job opportunities.

Persons who graduate with a bachelor's degree in economics through the year 2000 should face very keen competition for the limited number of economist positions for which they qualify. However, many will find employment in government, industry, and business as management or sales trainees, or as research or administrative assistants. Those with strong backgrounds in mathematics, statistics, survey design, and computer science may be hired by private firms for market research work. Those who meet State certification requirements may become high school economics teachers. (For additional information, see the statement on secondary school teachers elsewhere in the Handbook.)

Candidates who hold master's degrees in economics face very strong competition, particularly for teaching positions in colleges and universities. However, some may gain positions in junior and community colleges. Those with a strong background in marketing and finance may have the best prospects in business, banking, advertising, and management consulting firms.

Ph.D.'s are likely to face competition for academic positions, although top graduates from leading universities should have little difficulty in acquiring teaching jobs. Some will have to accept jobs at smaller or lower paying institutions. Ph.D.'s should have favorable opportunities to work as economists in government, industry, educational and research organizations, and consulting firms.

EARNINGS

According to a 1990 salary survey,persons with a bachelor's degree in economics received an average starting salary of about $30,000 a year; in marketing and distribution, about $25,000.

Median annual earning of full-time economists were about $47,500.

The median base salary of business economists was 70,000 according to a survey by the National Association of Business Economists. Over one-fourth of those responding also had income from secondary employment. Economists in general administration and international economics commanded the highest salaries; those in market research and econometrics, the lowest. The highest paid business economists were in the securities and investment, retail and wholesale trade, and insurance industries; the lowest paid were in the education, nonprofit research organization, and real estate industries.

The Federal Government recognizes education and experience in certifying applicants for entry level positions. In general, the entrance salary for economists having a bachelor's degree average about $19,000 a year; however, those with superior academic records could begin at about $23,000. Those having a master's degree could qualify for positions at an annual salary of about $27,500. Those with a PH.D. could begin at about $33,500, while some individuals could start at $39,500. Economists in the Federal Government average around $48,000 a year.

RELATED OCCUPATIONS

Economists are concerned with understanding and interpreting financial matters, among other subjects. Others with jobs in this area include financial managers, financial analysts, accountants and auditors, underwriters, actuaries, securities and financial services sales workers, credit analysts, loan officers, and budget officers.

SOURCES OF ADDITIONAL INFORMATION

For information on schools offering graduate training in economics, contact:

American Economic Association, 1313 21st Ave. South, Nashville, TN 37212.

For information on careers in business ecomomics, contact:

National Association of Business Economists, 28349 Chagrin Blvd., Suite 201, Cleveland, OH 44122.

For information about careers and salaries in market research, contact:

American Marketing Association, 250 South Wacker Dr., Chicago, IL 60606.

For information about careers in noncollegiate academic institutions, contact:

Joint Council on Economic Education, 2 Park Ave., New York, NY 10016.

HOW TO TAKE A TEST

You have studied hard, long, and conscientiously.

With your official admission card in hand, and your heart pounding, you have been admitted to the examination room.

You note that there are several hundred other applicants in the examination room waiting to take the same test.

They all appear to be equally well prepared.

You know that nothing but your best effort will suffice. The "moment of truth" is at hand: you now have to demonstrate objectively, in writing, your knowledge of content and your understanding of subject matter.

You are fighting the most important battle of your life—to pass and/or score high on an examination which will determine your career and provide the economic basis for your livelihood.

What extra, special things should you know and should you do in taking the examination?

BEFORE THE TEST

YOUR PHYSICAL CONDITION IS IMPORTANT

If you are not well, you can't do your best work on tests. If you are half asleep, you can't do your best either. Here are some tips:

1. Get about the same amount of sleep you usually get. Don't stay up all night before the test, either partying or worrying—DON'T DO IT.
2. If you wear glasses, be sure to wear them when you go to take the test. This goes for hearing aids, too.
3. If you have any physical problems that may keep you from doing your best, be sure to tell the person giving the test. If you are sick or in poor health, you really cannot do your best on any test. You can always come back and take the test some other time.

AT THE TEST

EXAMINATION TECHNIQUES

1. Read the *general* instructions carefully. These are usually printed on the first page of the examination booklet. As a rule, these instructions refer to the timing of the examination; the fact that you should not start work until the signal and must stop work at a signal, etc. If there are any *special* instructions, such as a choice of questions to be answered, make sure that you note this instruction carefully.

2. When you are ready to start work on the examination, that is as soon as the signal has been given, read the instructions to each question booklet, underline any key words or phrases, such as *least, best, outline, describe,* and the like. In this way you will tend to answer as requested rather than discover on reviewing your paper that you *listed without describing,* that you selected the *worst* choice rather than the *best* choice, etc.

3. If the examination is of the objective or so-called multiple-choice type, that is, each question will also give a series of possible answers: A, B, C, or D, and you are called upon to select the best answer and write the letter next to that answer on your answer paper, it is advisable to start answering each question in turn. There may be anywhere from 50 to 100 such questions in the three or four hours allotted and you can see how much time would be taken if you read through all the questions before beginning to answer any. Furthermore, if you come across a question or a group of questions which you know would be difficult to answer, it would undoubtedly affect your handling of all the other questions.

4. If the examination is of the essay-type and contains but a few questions, it is a moot point as to whether you should read all the questions before starting to answer any one. Of course if you are given a choice, say five out of seven and the like, then it is essential to read all the questions so you can eliminate the two which are most difficult. If, however, you are asked to answer all the questions, there may be danger in trying to answer the easiest one first because you may find that you will spend too much time on it. The best technique is to answer the first question, then proceed to the second, etc.

5. Time your answers. Before the examination begins, write down the time it started, then add the time allowed for the examination and write down the time it must be completed, then divide the time available somewhat as follows:

    a. If 3 ½ hours are allowed, that would be 210 minutes. If you have 80 objective-type questions, that would be an average of about 2 ½ minutes per question. Allow yourself no more than 2 minutes per question, or a total of 160 minutes, which will permit about 50 minutes to review.

    b. If for the time allotment of 210 minutes, there are 7 essay questions to answer, that would average about 30 minutes a question. Give yourself only 25 minutes per question so that you have about 35 minutes to review.

6. The most important instruction is *to read each question* and make sure you know what is wanted. The second most important instruction is to *time yourself properly* so that you answer every question. The third most important instruction is to *answer every question*. Guess if you have to but include something for each question, Remember that you will receive no credit for a blank and will probably receive some credit if you write something in answer to an essay question. If you guess a letter, say "B" for a multiple-choice question, you may have guessed right. If you leave a blank as the answer to a multiple-choice question, the examiners may respect your feelings but it will not add a point to your score. Some exams may penalize you for wrong answers, so in such cases *only*, you may not want to guess unless you have some basis for your answer.

7. Suggestions

   a. Objective-Type Questions

      (1) Examine the question booklet for proper sequence of pages and questions.

      (2) Read all instructions carefully.

      (3) Skip any question which seems too difficult; return to it after all other questions have been answered.

      (4) Apportion your time properly; do not spend too much time on any single question or group of questions.

      (5) Note and underline key words—*all, most, fewest, least, best, worst, same, opposite.*

      (6) Pay particular attention to negatives.

      (7) Note unusual option, e.g., unduly long, short, complex, different or similar in content to the body of the question.

      (8) Observe the use of "hedging" words—*probably, may, most likely, etc.*

      (9) Make sure that your answer is put next to the same number as the question.

      (10) Do not second guess unless you have good reason to believe the second answer is definitely more correct.

      (11) Cross out original answer if you decide another answer is more accurate; do not erase, *until* you are ready to hand your paper in.

      (12) Answer all questions; guess unless instructed otherwise.

      (13) Leave time for review.

b. Essay-Type Questions

(1) Read each question carefully.

(2) Determine exactly what is wanted. Underline key words or phrases.

(3) Decide on outline or paragraph answer.

(4) Include many different points and elements unless asked to develop any one or two points or elements.

(5) Show impartiality by giving pros and cons unless directed to select one side only.

(6) Make and write down any assumptions you find necessary to answer the question.

(7) Watch your English, grammar, punctuation, choice of words.

(8) Time your answers; don't crowd material.

8. Answering the Essay Question

Most essay questions can be answered by framing the specific response around several key words or ideas. Here are a few such key words or ideas:

M's: manpower, materials, methods, money, management

P's: purpose, program, policy, plan, procedure, practice, problems, pitfalls, personnel, public relations

a. Six basic steps in handling problems:

(1) preliminary plan and background development

(2) collect information, data and facts

(3) analyze and interpret information, data and facts

(4) analyze and develop solutions as well as make recommendations

(5) prepare report and sell recommendations

(6) install recommendations and follow up effectiveness

b. Pitfalls to Avoid

(1) *Taking Things for Granted*
A statement of the situation does not necessarily imply that each of the elements is necessarily true; for example, a complaint may be invalid and biased so that all that can be taken for granted is that a complaint has been registered

(2) *Considering only one side of a situation*
Wherever possible, indicate several alternatives and then point out the reasons you selected the best one.

(3) *Failing to indicate follow up*
Whenever your answer indicates action on your part, make certain that you will take proper follow-up action to see how successful your recommendations; procedures, or actions turn out to be.

(4) *Taking too long in answering any single question*
Remember to time your answers properly.

EXAMINATION SECTION

EXAMINATION SECTION

TEST 1

DIRECTIONS: Each question or incomplete statement is followed by several suggested answers or completions. Select the one that BEST answers the question or completes the statement. *PRINT THE LETTER OF THE CORRECT ANSWER IN THE SPACE AT THE RIGHT.*

1. In the economy of the United States, the actual gross national product is *most likely* to be less than the potential GNP at full capacity whenever 1.___
   A. business investment is large
   B. consumer spending is rising
   C. government spending is falling
   D. total spending is falling

2. _____ would tend to reduce consumer spending. 2.___
   A. A reduction in personal income tax rates
   B. A decline in consumer incomes
   C. An expectation that prices will soon rise
   D. Increased government payments to individuals

3. When the economy fluctuates between boom and depression, the part of *total* spending that changes by the largest percent is 3.___
   A. spending by families on consumer goods and services
   B. business spending on factories, machinery, and inventories
   C. state and local government spending on all activities
   D. business spending on wages and salaries

4. If, when there is full employment, the federal government increases its spending WITHOUT increasing its tax revenues, *generally* 4.___
   A. a serious depression will occur
   B. an increase in unemployment will occur
   C. the national debt will decrease
   D. inflation will occur

5. A government budgetary deficit exists whenever 5.___
   A. the national debt is decreasing
   B. taxes are reduced
   C. government expenditures are increased
   D. total government spending exceeds receipts

6. When more money is created through government mints or through increased bank lending, the result is *generally* 6.___
   A. more spending
   B. less spending
   C. higher interest rates
   D. decreased savings

7. The Federal Reserve Board *generally* tries to increase the money supply when it wants to 7.____
   A. fight unemployment during recessions
   B. fight inflation
   C. hold down the government debt
   D. make large profits

8. The limit of an economy's real output at any time is set by 8.____
   A. business demand for goods and services
   B. the quantity and quality of labor, capital, and natural resources
   C. government regulations and spending
   D. the amount of money in circulation

9. MOST of the funds on deposit in commercial banks originate through 9.____
   A. individuals depositing currency in banks
   B. the rise of our gold stock
   C. business firms extending credit to customers
   D. banks making loans and investments

10. A monetary policy is *often* ineffective when used to check a recession, because at such times 10.____
   A. banks lack reserves to make loans
   B. there may NOT be a strong demand for loans
   C. the Federal Reserve CANNOT engage in open-market conditions
   D. reserve requirements CANNOT be lowered

11. Rapidly growing economies differ from slowly growing economies in that the former are always characterized by a(n) 11.____
   A. slow rate of population growth
   B. abundant supply of natural resources
   C. high rate of investment
   D. balanced national budget

12. If effective demand (i.e., total spending) periodically falls short of productive capacity, the rate of growth of the economy over a long period will be _____ because 12.____
   A. higher; inefficient plants, equipment, and labor no longer need be employed
   B. higher; production will be concentrated on necessary goods rather than luxuries
   C. lower; some productive resources will not be employed
   D. lower; of a heavier reliance on the raw materials of foreign countries

13. Three of these statements are TRUE of the so-called under-developed economies. Which one is NOT? 13.____
   A. Approximately two-thirds of the world's population live in such areas.
   B. These areas would soon achieve developed economies if their domestic money supply could be greatly increased.

C. Low income in these areas makes savings for economic growth difficult.
D. Political and social conditions exist that hold back their economic development.

14. *Americans are a mixed-up people with no sense of ethical values. Everyone knows that baseball is far less necessary than food and steel, yet they pay ballplayers a lot more than farmers and steelworkers.* 14.____
Why?
A. Ballplayers are *really* entertainers rather than producers.
B. Ballplayers are more skilled than persons who get less pay.
C. Excellent baseball players are scarcer relative to the demand for their services.
D. There are fewer professional ballplayers than farmers or steelworkers.

15. The average annual family income before taxes in the United States in 1993 was between ____ and ____. 15.____
A. $10,000; $15,000 B. $15,000; $20,000
C. $20,000; $40,000 D. $40,000; $60,000

16. In the United States, the high wages received by MOST workers depend *largely* on 16.____
A. actions of the federal government
B. the social responsibility shown by business
C. our minimum wage laws
D. the high output per worker

17. Labor unions in the United States have 17.____
A. strengthened the bargaining position of laborers in relation to their employers
B. substantially increased the real wages of organized labor as compared with those of unorganized labor
C. increased the percent of Americans who earn their living by rendering labor services
D. increased competition in the labor market

18. The government program for agriculture is BEST summarized in which statement? 18.____
A. Output has been drastically reduced so that surpluses have not accumulated; thus, farm income and prices of farm products have been high.
B. An attempt has been made to improve farm incomes by taking a variety of measures to raise the price of farm products above the free market price.
C. The government pays farmers enough money to bring their yearly incomes after taxes up to the level of incomes received by average non-farm laborers.
D. Ours has been a policy of laissez-faire - of expressing concern for the farmer but generally doing nothing to affect the level of his income.

19. Identify the FALSE explanation of the *farm problem* in the United States. 19.____
   A. The growth of agricultural productivity has been much less rapid than that of the rest of the economy.
   B. Technological change has made it economical to use less labor and more capital in agriculture.
   C. As our economy has grown, the total demand for agricultural products has increased much less than for industrial products.
   D. When farm prices fall, the consumption of agricultural products increases only slightly.

20. Of these features of capitalism, communism as practiced in the former Soviet Union functioned without 20.____
   A. prices
   B. capital goods
   C. private profit
   D. all of the above

21. Which point is characteristic of both communism as practiced in the U.S.S.R. and private enterprise as practiced in the United States? 21.____
   A. Nearly all capital goods and natural resources are owned by the state.
   B. Trade unions have an important role in setting wages and conditions of work.
   C. Market prices automatically reflect consumer demand.
   D. Differences in money wages and salaries are used as an economic incentive.

22. As compared with more orthodox communism, democratic socialism (e.g., in the United Kingdom, Sweden, and India) 22.____
   A. has more extensive government control over wages
   B. uses wage incentives more for workers
   C. places more emphasis on rapid economic growth
   D. permits the people more influence over what is produced

Questions 23-25.

DIRECTIONS: Questions 23 to 25 refer to the following three charts.

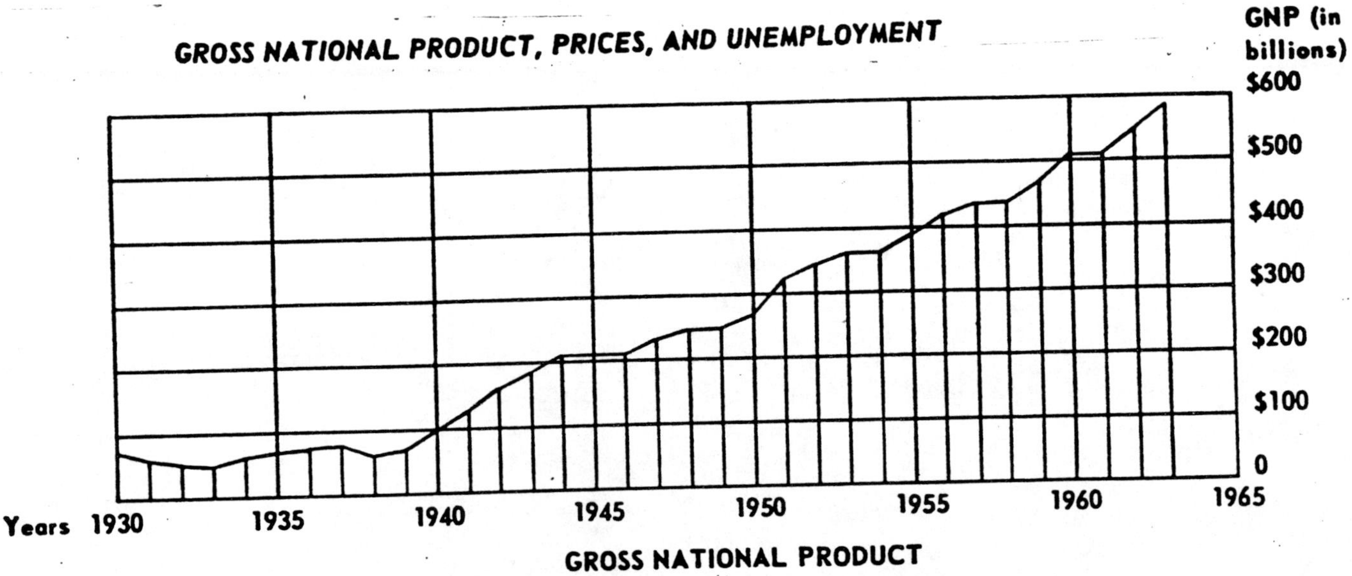

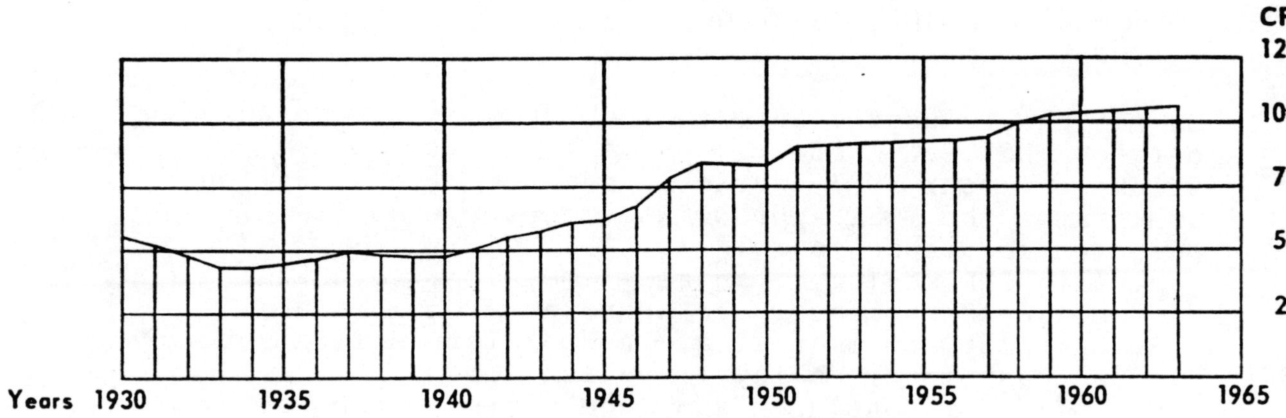

CONSUMER PRICE INDEX

(1957-59 = 100)

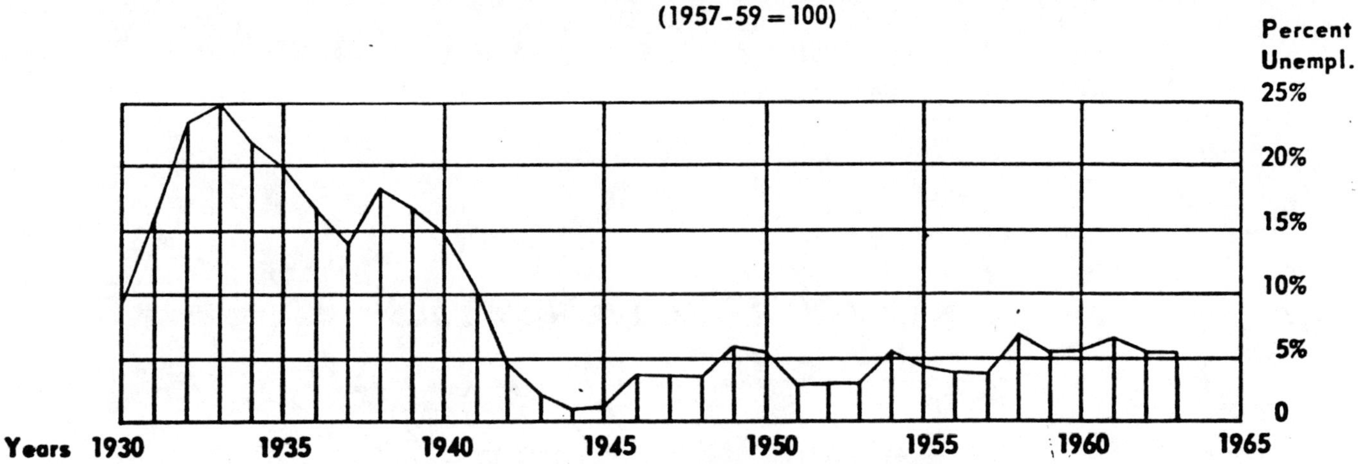

UNEMPLOYMENT

(Percent of civilian labor force)

Source: *Economic Report of the President, 1964*

23. Judging from your inspection of the charts above, the MOST serious economic problem of the early 1960's seems to be the   23.____
   A. decline in the output of the economy
   B. rapid inflation
   C. unemployment
   D. increase of the gross national product to a new all-time high

24. The fact that the consumer price index on the chart was *approximately* 75 in 1947 means that the average price of consumer goods and services in 1947 was about 24.____
   A. 75¢ a unit
   B. 75% above the average level of prices since 1947
   C. 25% less than 1957-59 prices
   D. 75% lower than at present

25. On the charts above, note the behavior of the economy between 1956 and 1958. 25.____
Which statement MOST correctly analyzes the situation and states the MOST appropriate monetary and fiscal policies for these years?
   A. With GNP moving to an all-time high, *no* change in policy is necessary to keep the economy stable.
   B. Unemployment is rising. A budgetary deficit and/or an easy money policy is called for.
   C. Inflation continues and accelerates. A budgetary surplus and/or a tight money policy is called for.
   D. A dilemma exists. The appropriate monetary-fiscal policy to reduce unemployment is *likely* to increase the inflation, and policies to check inflation may increase unemployment.

KEY (CORRECT ANSWERS)

1. D
2. B
3. B
4. D
5. D

6. A
7. A
8. B
9. D
10. B

11. C
12. C
13. B
14. C
15. C

16. D
17. A
18. B
19. A
20. C

21. D
22. D
23. C
24. C
25. D

TEST 2

DIRECTIONS: Each question or incomplete statement is followed by several suggested answers or completions. Select the one that BEST answers the question or completes the statement. *PRINT THE LETTER OF THE CORRECT ANSWER IN THE SPACE AT THE RIGHT.*

1. When a nation's human and material resources are being fully and efficiently used, more of any one product 1.____
   A. cannot be produced
   B. cannot be produced unless private enterprise rather than government does so
   C. can be produced only if there is less production of some other products
   D. can be produced only if there is a general decrease in prices

2. All economic systems (capitalist, communist, feudal, or any other) face similar economic problems. 2.____
   Which one of these questions would SOME but not all economies face?
   A. What will be produced and how?
   B. How can markets be kept competitive?
   C. How many resources will be devoted to maintaining and increasing future capacity?
   D. For whom will the goods be produced?

3. In a basically private enterprise economy, which group exercises the PRINCIPAL influence on the choice of goods produced over a long period of time? 3.____
   A. Consumers
   B. Government
   C. Big business
   D. Labor unions

4. Which is NOT a function of profits in a basically private enterprise economy? 4.____
   A. Providing an incentive for efficient production by businesses
   B. Rewarding producers who give consumers what they demand
   C. Inducing businessmen to assume necessary business risks
   D. Indicating to the government where wages are too low

5. How does a family's saving MOST clearly influence capital formation? 5.____
   A. Saving means spending less; therefore, family saving hurts the seller and thus discourages capital formation.
   B. Savings are ALWAYS invested by the saver; therefore, an increase in family saving increases capital formation.
   C. A family's savings are normally channeled through financial institutions to firms that *usually* use the savings for capital formation.
   D. A family's savings lead to capital formation when they are used to pay off debts.

6. In a basically private enterprise economy, the MAIN objective of businessmen is to 6.____
   A. provide good jobs for workers at reasonable wages
   B. secure government regulation that is favorable to business
   C. try to make profits
   D. provide highest-quality products

7. If a consumer is to exercise his freedom of choice wisely in a private enterprise economy, he 7.____
   A. should know whether a product was produced by a monopolist
   B. MUST know where products are produced so that he may purchase those made locally, if possible
   C. should know what alternative goods and services are available as well as their qualities and prices
   D. MUST have sufficient income to permit him to purchase whatever he chooses

8. Assume that the demand increases for a commodity produced by many competitive firms. 8.____
   The resulting rise in price of the commodity will *usually* lead to
   A. less being produced
   B. more being produced
   C. no change in production
   D. elimination of inefficient businesses from the market

9. If the supply of a commodity increases at the same time the demand for it falls, in the absence of counteracting forces, its price will 9.____
   A. rise B. fall
   C. stay the same D. be indeterminate

10. In a private enterprise economy, the public interest is served even when individuals pursue their own private economic goals. 10.____
   This is because of
   A. the social responsibility of private businessmen
   B. careful planning and coordination of economic activity
   C. the operation of competitive markets
   D. individuals who understand what is in the public interest

11. Under a private enterprise economy, the function of competition is to 11.____
   A. eliminate wasteful advertising
   B. eliminate interest and profits
   C. prevent large firms from driving small ones out of business
   D. force prices to the LOWEST level consistent with a reasonable profit

12. Of these factors, a(n) _____ is *not likely* to increase the demand for bricks. 12.____
   A. increase in the price of home construction
   B. increase in the incomes of potential home builders
   C. decrease in the price of mortar (i.e., a complementary commodity)
   D. increase in the price of lumber (i.e., a substitute for bricks)

13. Which of the following is the MOST basic economic objection to monopolies? 13.____
   A. Prices set by monopolies are *usually* too low.
   B. Monopolies exert disproportionate political power.
   C. When a monopoly fails, the effect upon our economy is far more serious than when a competitive enterprise fails.
   D. Economic resources will tend to be less efficiently allocated.

14. Identify the FALSE statement regarding the economy of the United States over the past fifty years. 14.____
   A. Monopoly has increased to the point where it controls more than half of our production.
   B. The average size of firms has grown substantially.
   C. Small firms and large firms have both increased in number.
   D. Improved transportation and communication have resulted in firms competing over larger markets.

15. The federal government attempts to eliminate monopolies MAINLY in order to 15.____
   A. ensure competition
   B. prevent small firms from decreasing
   C. expand public utilities
   D. prevent the growth of big business

16. In large business corporations, the common stockholders *generally* do NOT 16.____
   A. own the business
   B. receive a share of the profits
   C. vote for the board of directors
   D. manage the day-to-day business

17. The opportunity cost (or alternative cost) of a new public high school is the 17.____
   A. money cost of the new building
   B. other desirable economic goods that must be forgone to secure the school
   C. necessary increase in the annual tax rate
   D. cost of constructing it now as opposed to the cost of a new school at a later date

18. Government expenditures (federal, state, and local combined) *now* represent about what portion of the gross national product? 18.____
   A. A tenth
   B. A quarter
   C. Half
   D. Three-fourths

19. The bulk of federal government expenditure during the Reagan-Bush years was for 19.____
A. foreign aid
B. the space program
C. special benefits for the poor and unemployed
D. national defense

20. In a basically private enterprise economy, a(n) _____ is *likely* to alter MOST the pattern of consumer choice among alternative products. 20.____
A. general sales tax
B. personal income tax
C. excise tax on particular products
D. tax on business profits

21. Specialization and exchange within a nation or between nations create which effect? 21.____
A. A larger total quantity of wanted goods and services can be produced.
B. The independence of both nations and individuals is increased.
C. The danger of economic instability is reduced.
D. All costs of production will rise, but not proportionately.

22. When a nation is running a deficit in its international balance of payments, it is ALWAYS currently 22.____
A. exporting more goods than it is importing
B. importing more goods than it is exporting
C. paying more to other nations than others are paying to it
D. helping less fortunate nations to develop economically

23. Reduced U.S. tariffs would *probably* 23.____
A. lessen job opportunities in our export industries
B. injure most farmers
C. force some workers out of jobs in presently protected industries
D. lower the average U.S. standard of living

24. When obtained at various intervals, which one of these four types of statistics will give the BEST measure of the economic growth of a nation? 24.____
A. Balance of payments
B. Index of stock prices
C. Total employment
D. Real income per capita

25. Annual gross national product is a measure of 25.____
A. the quantity of goods and services produced by private businesses
B. the value of a nation's total output of goods and services
C. the price level of goods and services sold
D. that part of production which is used by the government

KEY (CORRECT ANSWERS)

1. C
2. B
3. A
4. D
5. C

6. C
7. C
8. B
9. B
10. C

11. D
12. A
13. D
14. A
15. A

16. D
17. B
18. B
19. D
20. C

21. A
22. C
23. C
24. D
25. B

TEST 3

DIRECTIONS: Each question or incomplete statement is followed by several suggested answers or completions. Select the one that BEST answers the question or completes the statement. *PRINT THE LETTER OF THE CORRECT ANSWER IN THE SPACE AT THE RIGHT.*

1. The MAXIMUM gross national product a nation can produce in any one year is set by 1.____
   A. its natural resources
   B. families' demand for products
   C. the amount of money people have to spend
   D. its productive resources

2. Often an economy operates at less than full employment. This is *most likely* to occur when 2.____
   A. total spending is inadequate
   B. there is inflation
   C. there is a scarcity of unskilled labor
   D. ever competition is intense

3. The *total* output of the economy is bought by which large group of spenders? 3.____
   A. Farmers, laborers, and housewives
   B. Consumers, business firms, and governments
   C. Investors, speculators, and bankers
   D. Corporations, households, and capitalists

4. In recessions in the United States since World War II, ______ has declined MOST sharply. 4.____
   A. family spending on consumer goods
   B. business firms' spending on plants, equipment, and inventories
   C. family spending on services
   D. government spending on goods and services

5. Increasing the government budgetary surplus or decreasing the deficit is particularly desirable in a period of 5.____
   A. inflation
   B. mass unemployment
   C. depression
   D. economic instability

6. The PRIMARY reason for the growth in federal debt over the last century has been government deficits caused by 6.____
   A. wasteful domestic expenditures and social welfare payments
   B. depressions and recessions
   C. declining tax receipts
   D. wars

7. An increase in the amount of money in the nation *usually* leads to higher prices EXCEPT when 7.____
   A. there is widespread unemployment of men and machines
   B. labor unions are strong
   C. the nation's gold reserves are adequate
   D. there is general prosperity

8. When commercial banks increase their loans to businesses and consumers, the result is a(n) 8.____
   A. decrease in the spending power of consumers and businesses
   B. increase in the nation's money supply
   C. increase in government control over the economy
   D. increase in the banks' excess reserves

9. In an inflationary period, an *appropriate* policy for the Federal Reserve would be to 9.____
   A. sell government securities on the open market
   B. lower legal reserve requirements
   C. decrease the discount rate
   D. encourage member banks to increase their loans

10. _____ are typically hurt the MOST by inflation. 10.____
    A. Farmers
    B. Debtors
    C. Government bondholders
    D. Businessmen

11. Assume our economy is operating at full capacity. Which policy would NOT be appropriate to increase our rate of economic growth? 11.____
    A. Encouraging an increase of private savings and investment in capital goods and equipment
    B. Improving the skill and knowledge of people through increased education
    C. Developing technology and managerial ability
    D. Encouraging an increase in personal consumption

12. If total demand declines relative to the productive capacity of the economy, 12.____
    A. the growth rate is *likely* to slow down, at least temporarily
    B. inflation is *likely* to occur
    C. a large government budgetary surplus is *likely* to occur
    D. employment is *likely* to increase

13. The average per capita income of the two-thirds of the world's population in the so-called underdeveloped nations is _____ of ours. 13.____
    A. less than one-tenth
    B. about one-quarter
    C. about one-half
    D. about three-fourths

14. The MOST general cause of low individual incomes in the United States is 14.____
    A. lack of valuable productive services to sell
    B. unwillingness to work
    C. automation
    D. discrimination against non-union employees

15. In the United States during the present century, 15.____
  A. inequality in personal incomes has been *largely* eliminated
  B. the rich have become richer and the poor poorer
  C. average real family income after taxes has remained *generally* unchanged
  D. income inequality has been *somewhat* reduced

16. High wages in the United States are based on the high productivity of U.S. labor. 16.____
All of these factors contribute to this high productivity EXCEPT
  A. the skill and work habits of U.S. labor
  B. our accumulation of a large stock of capital goods
  C. our technological and managerial advances
  D. tariff protection from competition of low-paid foreign workers

17. Both featherbedding by unions and monopolistic practices by employers are *likely* to result in 17.____
  A. an increase in average labor productivity for the nation as a whole
  B. a less efficient use of resources
  C. less labor being used in the industry affected
  D. a raising of average real wages in the nation as a whole

18. Identify the MOST obvious result of our governmental policy toward agriculture. 18.____
  A. The average farm income has been raised *almost* to the level of the average non-farm income.
  B. Large surpluses of farm commodities have been accumulated by the government.
  C. Capital and labor have turned to agriculture to take advantage of guaranteed high prices and profits.
  D. The family farm has been *almost* completely replaced by the large corporate farm.

19. Measures to increase economic security against unemployment will tend to increase economic efficiency if 19.____
  A. one cannot transfer to better-paying jobs offered by other employers, to be eligible for benefits
  B. the security the measure provides tends to reduce one's incentive to produce
  C. the costs of the measures are borne equally by firms regardless of their record for causing economic insecurity
  D. the average output per worker is increased as a result of improved economic security

20. In the United States, in contrast to communist nations, 20.____
A. the problem of scarcity has been eliminated
B. consumer spending *largely* determines what commodities are produced
C. incomes are unequally distributed
D. government plays an insignificant role in economic life

21. The interest rate charged on overnight loans from one member bank of the Federal Reserve System to another is known as 21.____
A. overnight fund interest rate
B. ex-dividend rate
C. Federal funds rate
D. fiscal debenture reserve rate

22. Compared with the U.S. economy, the democratic socialist economies of the United Kingdom, the Scandinavian countries, and India 22.____
A. are considerably more productive
B. have more government ownership and control
C. demonstrate clearly that *only* private enterprise is compatible with democracy
D. have been short-lived, for in two of the cases socialism has been abandoned

Questions 23-25.

DIRECTIONS: Questions 23-25 refer to the charts on the on the following page.

23. We desire a growing economy in which the price level is stable and employment reasonably high. 23.____
The charts on the preceding page show that we have MOST fully approximated this ideal between ____ and ____.
A. 1937; 1938
B. 1940; 1941
C. 1946; 1947
D. 1955; 1956

24. Judging from your inspection of the three charts, the MOST serious economic problem of the immediate postwar period (1946-48) is 24.____
A. decline in the output of the economy
B. inflation
C. unemployment
D. declining output per worker

25. On the charts, note the behavior of the economy between 1950 and 1952. 25.____
Identify the statement which MOST correctly analyzes the situation and states the MOST appropriate monetary and fiscal policies for these years.
A. The GNP is moving to an all-time high and prices are stable; no change in policy is called for.
B. Unemployment is rising; a budgetary deficit and/or an easy money policy is called for.
C. It is a period of inflation; a budgetary surplus and/or a tight money policy is called for.
D. Employment is falling and prices are rising; therefore, a budgetary deficit and/or a tight money policy is called for.

Questions 23-25.

DIRECTIONS: Questions 23 to 25 refer to the following three charts.

GROSS NATIONAL PRODUCT, PRICES, AND UNEMPLOYMENT

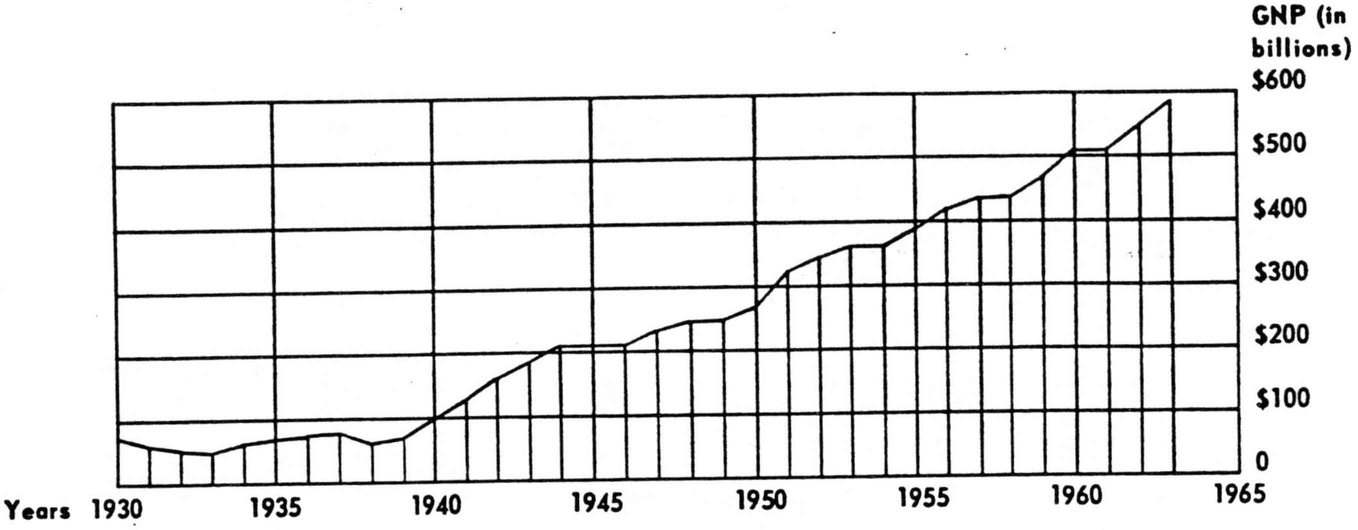

GROSS NATIONAL PRODUCT

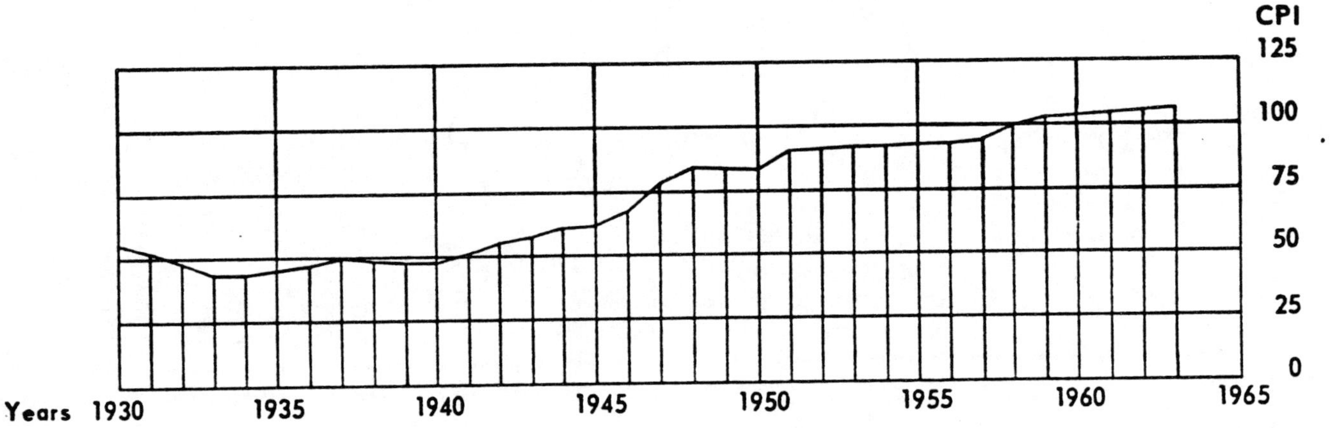

CONSUMER PRICE INDEX

(1957-59 = 100)

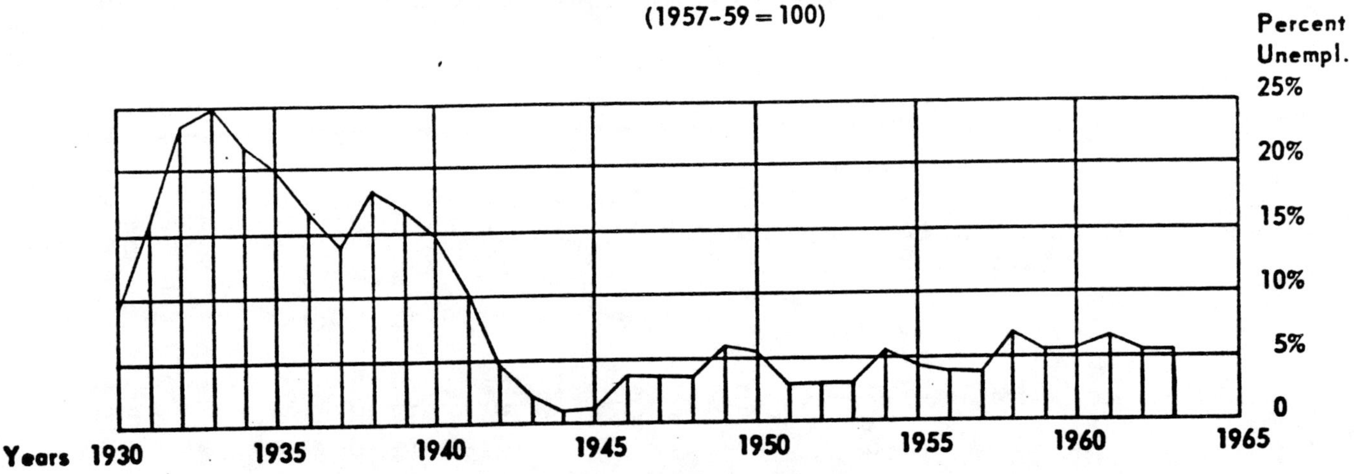

UNEMPLOYMENT

(Percent of civilian labor force)

KEY (CORRECT ANSWERS)

1. D
2. A
3. B
4. B
5. A

6. D
7. A
8. B
9. A
10. C

11. D
12. A
13. A
14. A
15. D

16. D
17. B
18. B
19. D
20. B

21. C
22. B
23. D
24. B
25. C

TEST 4

DIRECTIONS: Each question or incomplete statement is followed by several suggested answers or completions. Select the one that BEST answers the question or completes the statement. *PRINT THE LETTER OF THE CORRECT ANSWER IN THE SPACE AT THE RIGHT.*

1. Every economic system faces the need to economize. In this context, the BEST definition of *to economize* is to 1.___
   A. save money and thus reduce the national debt
   B. dispense with the production of luxuries
   C. balance the government's budget by reducing spending
   D. make the best use of scarce resources that have alternative uses

2. What is meant by the assertion that *every* economic system (such as socialism, capitalism, communism) faces the fact of scarcity? 2.___
   A. There are insufficient productive resources to satisfy all wants of a society.
   B. There are times when some products can be had *only* by paying high prices.
   C. In the beginning, every society faces shortages, but a mature economy, such as our own, overcomes scarcity in time.
   D. All economies have depressions during which scarcities exist.

3. Which point BEST characterizes the relation between producers, consumers, and government in a private enterprise economy? 3.___
   A. Producers decide what to produce, government how it shall be produced, and consumers who shall receive the product.
   B. Consumer spending leads producers to decide what shall be produced and how resources shall be used. Government seeks to maintain competition and the rights of private property.
   C. Consumers decide what should be produced, producers how BEST to produce it, and government who shall receive which products.
   D. Government ultimately decides what shall be produced and how. Consumers and producers, as voters, control the government.

4. Three of the following are essential to the operation of a private enterprise economy. Which one might such an economy operate WITHOUT? 4.___
   A. Profit motive
   B. Markets
   C. Corporations
   D. Prices

5. The principle of diminishing returns is BEST illustrated by 5.____
   A. small firms being driven out of business by large firms
   B. any decline in the average rate of profits
   C. a slowing rate of increase in output as a farmer adds increasing amounts of fertilizer to his land
   D. the decline in personal income as workers age

6. Business firms wish to sell their products at a high price; households wish to buy products at low prices. In a private enterprise economy, this conflict of interests 6.____
   A. is reconciled by competitive markets
   B. is reconciled by government regulation
   C. does NOT exist; there is really *no* conflict of interest between households and firms
   D. is NOT reconciled; since all household heads are members of firms, the interests of firms prevail

7. In a private enterprise economy, government encourages freedom of choice by 7.____
   A. guaranteeing complete freedom of choice to households and firms
   B. limiting this freedom for some if their choices might reduce freedom of choice significantly for others
   C. requiring individuals and firms to use their freedom of choice wisely
   D. seeing that individuals and firms choose what the majority believes BEST

8. A rise in the price of ____ would be *likely* to increase the demand for butter. 8.____
   A. butter
   B. oleomargarine
   C. bread
   D. any of the above

9. Assuming that the supply of a product remains constant as the demand for it increases, its price will *normally* 9.____
   A. fall
   B. rise
   C. stay the same
   D. either rise or fall

10. ______ is MOST essential for a private enterprise economy. 10.____
   A. Active competition in the marketplace
   B. The functioning of labor unions
   C. Action by responsible business leaders
   D. Extensive government regulation

11. The price of shoes is *likely* to be increased by 11.____
   A. more capital investment by producers
   B. a decrease in the demand for shoes
   C. a decrease in the supply of shoes
   D. new machines reducing the cost of shoe production

12. If the government were to levy a tax of one dollar on every pair of shoes sold, a *most likely* result would be that 12.____
    A. consumers would pay a higher price for shoes and probably buy a smaller quantity
    B. suppliers would increase the quantity sold in order to offset the taxes paid to the government
    C. consumers would pay a higher price and, as a result, suppliers would make larger profits
    D. suppliers would sell more and charge a higher price

13. *Generally*, when a monopoly replaces private competitive enterprises, 13.____
    A. production efficiency is increased because of the larger scale of operation
    B. the market *no* longer tends to bring about the MOST efficient allocation of resources
    C. there is an increase in the number of firms making the product
    D. the monopolist controls both consumers and labor

14. The purpose of the Sherman and Clayton Antitrust Acts is to 14.____
    A. keep markets effectively competitive
    B. keep firms from becoming large
    C. prevent banks from becoming trusts
    D. protect the investing public

15. Common stocks, limited liability, and a charter are characteristic of 15.____
    A. individual proprietorships
    B. partnerships
    C. private business corporations
    D. most small business firms

16. Over the past fifty years, the share of the total U.S. market controlled by the hundred largest firms has 16.____
    A. changed by only a small amount
    B. risen substantially
    C. increased to more than 90 percent
    D. fallen steadily

17. These arguments have been used regarding the proposals for increased public expenditures on education. Which one shows the BEST use of economic reasoning, using the alternative (or opportunity cost) principle? 17.____
    A. Taxpayers should compare the probable sacrifices resulting from the added tax with the probable advantages of the new program.
    B. In real terms, the added school tax will cost us necessary food and clothing, adequate support of our churches, and essential medical care.
    C. Luxuries are the real alternative cost of the proposed educational improvements.
    D. Whenever a product is good, public or private expenditure on it is always desirable.

18. Government expenditure (federal, state, and local combined) is now the GREATEST for 18.____
 A. social services, including health and social security
 B. salaries of elected public officials, upkeep of public buildings, and cost of hearings, of the court system, and of highways
 C. public education - elementary, secondary, and higher
 D. national defense and related operations

19. Most taxes divert spending power; as a result, control over some resources passes from 19.____
 A. the government to individuals and businesses
 B. individuals and businesses to government
 C. the federal government to the state government
 D. gross national product to national income

20. Given our present pattern of government expenditure, the graduated or progressive income tax causes 20.____
 A. income after taxes to be more evenly distributed
 B. the rich to get richer and the poor to get poorer
 C. wage earners to pay more tax than property owners
 D. it to be impossible to inherit wealth

21. Specialization and division of labor by nations followed by increasing international trade *probably* would 21.____
 A. increase total world production of wanted goods and services
 B. lower living standards in the wealthy nations
 C. increase the likelihood of worldwide unemployment
 D. eliminate differences in standards of living among nations

22. A nation has a deficit in its international balance of payments when it 22.____
 A. buys more goods and services abroad than it sells
 B. makes more payments, excluding gold, to other countries than it receives from them
 C. has an unfavorable balance of trade
 D. owes more gold to other nations than it has

23. Each statement about tariffs is *likely* to be TRUE EXCEPT that tariffs 23.____
 A. preserve employment in domestic industries whose products they protect
 B. reduce the market for our exports by reducing our imports
 C. encourage the growth of our most efficient industries and eliminate the least efficient
 D. benefit some groups at the expense of the national standard of living

24. Inflation is *most likely* to benefit 24.____
 A. savings bank depositors
 B. debtors
 C. life insurance policyholders
 D. persons living on fixed pensions

25. The BEST single measure of the total economic output in the United States is the 25.____
A. gross national product
B. total amount of take-home pay
C. consumer price index
D. index of industrial production

KEY (CORRECT ANSWERS)

1. D
2. A
3. B
4. C
5. C

6. A
7. B
8. B
9. B
10. A

11. C
12. A
13. B
14. A
15. C

16. A
17. A
18. D
19. B
20. A

21. A
22. B
23. C
24. B
25. A

ECONOMICS

EXAMINATION SECTION

TEST 1

DIRECTIONS: Each question or incomplete statement is followed by several suggested answers or completions. Select the one that BEST answers the question or completes the statement. *PRINT THE LETTER OF THE CORRECT ANSWER IN THE SPACE AT THE RIGHT.*

1. The following is a complete and correct definition of the demand curve for commodity X. It shows, for a given market, 1.___
   A. how much X will be bought at the equilibrium price
   B. how, as people's incomes rise and they have more money to spend, their purchases of X will increase, and by how much
   C. how the amount of money people spend to purchase X changes as the price they must pay for it changes
   D. the amounts of X that will be bought each period, at each and any price, assuming other factors influencing demand (income, tastes, etc.) remain constant
   E. the amounts of X to be supplied in each period, at each and any price, assuming other factors influencing sale remain constant

2. *A change in quantity demanded* (as distinct from *a change in demand*) means 2.___
   A. that buyers have decided to buy more (or less) than they are now buying, at the existing price
   B. the same thing as a change in demand
   C. a change in purchases resulting from some shift in the supply curve
   D. that the demand curve must have shifted in position
   E. that the demand curve has become more elastic than it previously was

3. If the demand for any product is described as *elastic* (or *price-elastic*), it means specifically that 3.___
   A. it would be possible to sell more of the product than is now being sold at the present price
   B. with any increase in consumer income, buyers would buy substantially more than they are now buying
   C. following any reduction in price, consumers would buy a greater quantity of the product than they are now buying
   D. if supply were to be increased for any reason, causing a fall in price, the total money outlay of consumers for the product would then decrease
   E. if supply were to be increased for any reason, causing a fall in price, the total money outlay of consumers for the product would then increase

4. If some commodity such as wheat is used as money in a society, then the amount of money (wheat) which a man will ask for a unit of some other good he has to sell will depend 4.___
   A. mainly upon the usefulness of wheat in feeding himself and his family
   B. upon the price of wheat in terms of gold or silver
   C. in no way upon the value of wheat, no matter how used
   D. upon the prices of still other goods which he may hope to buy
   E. upon his personal liking for, or dislike of, wheat as a food

5. If a commodity or substance is to be used successfully as money, the following (according to economists) is a necessary requirement: 5.___
   It must
   A. possess inherent value - i.e., must be useful for its own sake, independent of its use as money
   B. be backed by one of the precious metals, preferably gold
   C. be a free good
   D. carry the stamp of approval of some government
   E. none of the above

6. In terms of numbers, the form of business unit MOST frequently found in the United States today is the 6.___
   A. individual, or single, proprietorship
   B. partnership
   C. small corporation
   D. giant corporation
   E. none of the above

7. The term *limited liability* is frequently used in describing the characteristics of a corporation. 7.___
   It means the following:
   A. Any officer of the corporation is strictly limited in his ability to speak for the corporation and commit it to any liability
   B. Once a shareholder has paid for his stock, he has no further financial obligation, regardless of how much trouble the corporation gets into
   C. The corporation's liability to pay dividends to its stockholders is a limited one, since it is required to pay them only if it has earned a profit
   D. There are certain obligations which a corporation can legally refuse to pay
   E. The corporation has only a limited obligation to meet claims made by any single person or firm against it (provided it has acted within the scope of its charter), so that there is some protection for its assets and financial position

8. A corporation's obligation to pay interest on bonds it has issued is PROPERLY described as follows: 8.___
   A. Interest must be paid regardless of whether a profit has been earned or not
   B. Interest must be paid whenever a profit has been earned
   C. Interest need not be paid even if a profit has been earned, but it must be paid before any dividend is paid
   D. Normally interest ranks ahead of dividends, but there are some circumstances in which a dividend can be paid without payment of bond interest
   E. Interest ranks behind dividends and is paid only after dividends have been paid in full

9. The MAIN reason why indirect, or *capital-using*, methods of production have not displaced direct methods in economically underdeveloped areas of the world is that 9.___
   A. the governments of such areas have not issued enough money to finance indirect methods
   B. people do not realize that the indirect methods would produce more consumption goods
   C. there are no indirect methods that would actually produce more consumption goods
   D. such areas do not have a properly functioning price system
   E. the adoption of such indirect methods would involve a sacrifice of present consumption

10. The economic problem of how goods shall be produced is that of 10.___
   A. finding out how much product will be obtained when given quantities of factors of production are put to work together in the most effective known manner
   B. having a mechanism that will somehow reveal what goods people really want to be produced
   C. getting the existing factors of production distributed among different occupations to best produce whatever goods the community wants
   D. deciding how the goods that have been produced shall be distributed among the people who made those goods
   E. none of the above

11. If, with respect to the guns-and-butter-production-possibility diagram used in some books, the economy's actual output is marked by a point inside (to the south-west) of the production-possibility curve, this means that 11.___
   A. it is impossible to produce more guns without the sacrifice of some butter output
   B. either all available resources are not being fully employed or they are not being employed to the best advantage
   C. the law of diminishing returns cannot be in operation
   D. the diagram illustrates something which could not possibly happen
   E. the phenomenon of *increasing returns to scale* must be in operation

12. The law of diminishing returns notes the effect on output resulting from an increase in productive inputs. This effect depends on one assumption, without which the law does not apply.
The assumption is that 12.___
   A. although the output increase results from an increase in productive inputs, at least one such input must remain fixed in supply during the process
   B. the supply of all productive inputs must increase proportionately to produce the increase in output
   C. all productive inputs except one must be held fixed in supply, and only that one input may be allowed to increase
   D. as successive units of the productive input are added, the inherent quality of that input must decline
   E. the physical quantity of output may increase in proportion to the increase in inputs, but the worth of that output in the eyes of consumers must decline

13. The use of a money pricing system is NOT expected to help settle the following economic problem: 13.___
   A. Determining the particular output of goods and services that is best for a community to have, regardless of the tastes of any or all individual consumers therein
   B. Distribution of money income between different individuals in the community
   C. Helping a consumer with given tastes and a limited income to decide how best to spend that income
   D. How much of the total available resource supply is to be occupied in making any given consumer good
   E. The particular kinds of resources (factors of Production) that should be used for the manufacture of any given consumer good

14. The *law of downward-sloping demand* says the following: 14.___
   A. An excess of supply over demand will induce price reductions
   B. As price falls, people spend more money to buy the commodity in question
   C. When a demand schedule is illustrated graphically, it runs from northeast to southwest
   D. When price falls, quantity purchased normally increases
   E. None of these

15. In a system of free private enterprise, the following must consciously assume responsibility for deciding how the three basic economic problems - What, How, and For Whom - are to be settled: 15.___
   A. The law-making branch of the government
   B. The general public
   C. One or more administrative agencies of the government
   D. All business firms engaged in production
   E. None of the above

16. In the following table, circle the letter showing the interval in which demand is elastic. 16.___

	P	q
	1	100
A.	3	60
B.	8	30
C.	15	10
D.	30	5
E.	50	4

17. Using the same table as in the above problem, circle the letter showing the interval in which demand is of unitary elasticity. 17.___
A. A B. B C. C D. D E. E

18. Most of the very large U.S. federal debt outstanding arose as the result of 18.___
A. war
B. depressions
C. borrowing to meet interest charges on previous debt
D. borrowing from abroad
E. none of the above

19. The C plus I plus G schedule would tend to be shifted up by 19.___
A. an increase in taxes
B. a decrease in government spending
C. an increase in interest rates
D. open-market sales by the central bank
E. none of these

20. An expansionary monetary policy adopted by a central bank will be unsuccessful if 20.___
A. prices do not increase
B. saving on the part of the public does not decrease
C. investment spending is not changed by a change in the interest rate
D. the inflationary tendency which prompted this policy is not checked
E. no decrease in the price of government bonds occurs

21. If the Federal Reserve authorities wished to pursue an expansionary monetary policy, it would be CORRECT for them to 21.___
A. raise the Discount Rate to discourage hoarding by the public
B. raise reserve requirements to eliminate any excess reserves held by the Member banks
C. raise margin requirements to discourage wasteful speculation
D. sell securities on the open market to drive interest rates down
E. do none of the above

22. If the level of spending increases, with the quantity of money held constant, then 22.___
   A. the velocity of circulation of money must have increased
   B. the amount of real national output must have increased
   C. either the velocity of money circulation or the amount of real national output must have increased, or both
   D. the amount of real national output must have decreased
   E. either the velocity of money circulation must have increased, or the amount of real national output decreased, or both

23. One of the following statements is FALSE: 23.___
   A. Tax reduction tends to stimulate income
   B. Tax reduction tends to increase personal consumption
   C. Tax reduction tends to increase personal saving
   D. Whatever else tax reduction does, the increases in personal consumption resulting from tax reductions must stimulate income
   E. If tax reductions cause personal saving to increase, then Net National Product will fail

24. By *induced investment* is meant 24.___
   A. changes in investment which result from a change in Net National Product
   B. the fact that increased saving may sometimes result in increased investment
   C. investment made as a result of government orders
   D. an increase in investment which results from technological change
   E. none of the above

25. By the *Paradox of Thrift* is meant the fact that 25.___
   A. positive saving will always mean unemployment
   B. if changes in investment are induced by changes in Net National Product, then a decision on the part of people to save more might result in their actually saving less
   C. if the economy is at full employment, a decision on the part of people to save more might produce an inflationary gap
   D. saving stimulates investment spending so as to worsen an inflationary spiral
   E. saving must always equal investment

KEY (CORRECT ANSWERS)

1. D	6. A	11. B	16. C	21. E
2. C	7. B	12. A	17. D	22. A
3. E	8. A	13. A	18. C	23. E
4. D	9. E	14. D	19. E	24. A
5. E	10. E	15. E	20. B	25. B

TEST 2

DIRECTIONS: Each question or incomplete statement is followed by several suggested answers or completions. Select the one that BEST answers the question or completes the statement. *PRINT THE LETTER OF THE CORRECT ANSWER IN THE SPACE AT THE RIGHT.*

1. The calculation of Net National Product does NOT include 1.___
   A. net interest payments
   B. depreciation allowances
   C. rental income of individuals
   D. payments made to all government employees
   E. corporate profits before taxes

2. A stationary economy is one where 2.___
   A. no factories or machines are ever built
   B. the economy is growing but at a fixed rate instead of an accelerating one
   C. the economy is eating up its capital stock and is, therefore, not growing
   D. the capital stock is maintained at a steady level
   E. there can be no divergence of Gross National Product from Net National Product

3. The *propensity-to-consume* of families refers to the 3.___
   A. amounts of consumption expenditure associated with different levels of income
   B. fraction of an extra dollar of income that would be spent on consumption
   C. manner in which the family allocates its consumption on food, shelter, clothing, etc.
   D. manner in which the family would allocate extra dollars of income on food, clothing, etc.
   E. incentive of a family to obtain more income in order to spend more

4. If a family saves $10,000 of a $50,000 income and its propensity-to-consume function has the typical shape and position, then its marginal propensity to consume should be 4.___
   A. less than 4/5
   B. 4/5
   C. greater than 4/5 but less than 1
   D. equal to 1
   E. any of the above - impossible to tell from the data given

5. The value of the housekeeping service of a wife is excluded from Net National Product because 5.___
   A. it is a transfer item
   B. no money payment is involved and, therefore, it must be excluded
   C. it does not represent a current contribution to a factor of production
   D. of the problem of measurement
   E. of none of these

6. Government share of national product is HIGHEST in 6.___
   A. India B. Puerto Rico C. United Kingdom
   D. Japan E. United States

7. Government expenditures have been rising, but the rate of government expenditure to the increasing level of national income 7.___
   A. has been *remarkably* constant
   B. has shown generally a declining trend
   C. has shown a generally rising trend
   D. rose rapidly from 1975 to 1987, then declined
   E. none of these

8. One of the following industries would be much less vulnerable to the business cycle than the others: 8.___
   A. Food processing
   B. Building construction
   C. Shipbuilding
   D. Iron and steel manufacture
   E. None of these

9. By the *excess reserves* of a commercial bank is meant 9.___
   A. assets which, although not money, can be quickly converted into money by the bank should the need arise
   B. money and near-money assets possessed by the bank in excess of 100 percent of the amount of its demand deposits
   C. cash which must be kept on hand, not because the everyday needs of the bank demand it, but because of a legal requirement
   D. money held by the bank in excess of that fraction of its deposits which is required by law
   E. none of these

10. The economy's money supply will increase whenever commercial banks 10.___
    A. reduce their demand-deposit liabilities by paying out part of these accounts in the form of coins or bills
    B. increase their demand-deposit liabilities by receiving coins or bills from the public as a deposit
    C. withdraw part of their deposit with a Federal Reserve Bank
    D. increase their loans to the public
    E. none of these

11. If the Federal Reserve sells government bonds to the public on a large scale, the following is a LIKELY result: A(n) 11.___
    A. decrease in interest rates and a rise in total spending (unless spending fails to respond to easier credit conditions)
    B. rise in stock market prices as activity in this market responds to increased activity in the bond market
    C. increase in Reserve Bank credit
    D. contraction of bank reserves and a reduction in bank lending
    E. none of these

12. In a depression, when the Federal Reserve was trying to expand business activity, it would NOT 12.___
   A. raise the total of bank reserves
   B. expand the amount of Reserve Bank credit
   C. sell government bonds
   D. lower the legal reserve ratio required of banks with respect to their deposits
   E. none of these

13. Most governments would PROBABLY prefer 13.___
   A. unemployment to suppressed inflation
   B. suppressed inflation to unemployment
   C. open inflation to suppressed inflation
   D. open inflation to unemployment
   E. none of these

14. Effective demand as related to general employment may BEST be defined as 14.___
   A. greater demand for goods and services
   B. increased demand for higher wages
   C. desire for new and cheaper sources of raw materials
   D. quantity of labor that employers will hire at the prevailing wage rates
   E. none of these

15. According to principles of comparative advantage, 15.___
   A. trade is a substitute for international movement of productive factors
   B. the gains from international trade will be evenly divided among the trading nations
   C. a country with absolute advantage in two goods will not import either
   D. world total production of the traded goods is unaffected by trade, for the increases in output by exporters are just offset by the decreases on the part of the importers
   E. none of these

16. A sound economic argument can be advanced in favor of protective tariffs aimed at 16.___
   A. giving long-term support to an increasing-cost industry
   B. giving initial support to a decreasing-cost industry
   C. raising the general level of real wages by raising money wages in the protected industries
   D. equalizing the costs of production at home and abroad
   E. none of these

17. The International Monetary Fund 17.___
   A. provides long-term loans for development projects
   B. provides short-term credit to stabilize foreign exchange rates
   C. makes loans to foreigners for purchase of U.S. goods only
   D. is a central pool of gold and dollars earned and used by the British Commonwealth countries
   E. none of these

18. The trade policy MOST likely to promote industrialization in an overpopulated agricultural country today is 18.___
A. a tariff on manufactured goods with low initial rates gradually raised over the following years
B. a tariff on manufactured goods with high initial rates gradually reduced over the following years
C. a stable rate of tariff on agricultural imports
D. free trade
E. none of these

19. Devaluation of the currency by a given country tends directly to 19.___
A. reduce the physical volume of exports
B. raise the domestic selling price of imported goods
C. maintain the physical volume of imports for which demand elasticity is unity
D. decrease the burden of servicing the foreign debt
E. none of these

20. Expenditures of French tourists in the United States affect the French balance of payments in much the same way as 20.___
A. French imports from the United States
B. French exports to the United States
C. American tourists travelling in France
D. United States loans to France
E. none of these

21. According to the C.E.D. pamphlet on United States Tariff Policy, wherever an industry would be damaged by tariff reduction, government should 21.___
A. pay a subsidy to the firms in this industry
B. offer a bonus to displaced workers
C. promote diversification of industry
D. not cut the tariff
E. none of these

22. A factor which did NOT contribute to the Post World War II *dollar shortage* was 22.___
A. frequent depreciation of currencies by the dollar-shortage countries
B. wartime destruction of productive facilities in Europe and Asia
C. efforts by Europeans and Asians to live beyond their means
D. faster technological progress in dollar countries than elsewhere
E. none of these

23. A tariff for protection against the competition of cheap foreign labor provides a short-run benefit for 23.___
A. the protected workers B. all workers
C. all consumers D. unions
E. none of these

24. The following transfer payment is excluded from the computation of national income: 24.___
   A. payment for an intermediary good
   B. payment for a service rendered by a soldier to the government
   C. payment of interest on a government bond
   D. payment of interest on a General Motors bond
   E. undistributed corporation profits

25. *Liquidity preference* refers to the 25.___
   A. desire of banks to avoid long-term loans
   B. to the evaluation of cash as against other forms of asset holdings
   C. to the relationship between inventory holdings and the level of consumer demand
   D. the desire to liquidate ownership of producer durables and inventories in the face of declining consumption
   E. the rising trend in the consumption of alcoholic beverages

KEY (CORRECT ANSWERS)

1. B
2. D
3. B
4. C
5. B

6. C
7. C
8. A
9. D
10. D

11. D
12. C
13. B
14. D
15. B

16. B
17. B
18. B
19. B
20. A

21. C
22. A
23. A
24. A
25. B

TEST 3

DIRECTIONS: Each question or incomplete statement is followed by several suggested answers or completions. Select the one that BEST answers the question or completes the statement. *PRINT THE LETTER OF THE CORRECT ANSWER IN THE SPACE AT THE RIGHT.*

1. When the American Government borrowed in order to finance World War II, it thereby 1.___
   A. shifted the economic burden to future generations who would have to pay the interest and principal
   B. intensified the danger of national bankruptcy
   C. in no sense shifted the burden of the war on future generations
   D. placed the American people, though to a lesser degree, in the same difficult position as the British were placed by the war-time borrowing of their government from the United States and other foreign governments
   E. none of these

2. The existence of a large internally held public debt has 2.___
   A. no effect on the nation as a whole
   B. creates the danger of national bankruptcy
   C. has no effect on the nation as a whole, but does affect certain special interest groups
   D. is likely to depress the level of consumption and, hence, lower the equilibrium Net National Product
   E. is likely to make for greater inequality in the distribution of incomes and to dampen work incentive

3. In the course of production of goods by the modern corporation, marginal costs are those costs which 3.___
   A. are considered variable costs
   B. are considered fixed costs
   C. result from a one-unit addition to output
   D. are obtained by dividing the total cost of production by the number of units produced
   E. none of these

4. The MAJOR source of local and state tax revenue is ____ tax. 4.___
   A. the payroll
   B. highway (gasoline)
   C. sales
   D. individual and corporate income
   E. property

5. A rise in national income induces a further fall. This principal is associated with 5.___
   A. Joseph Schumpeter
   B. Alvin Hansen
   C. the accelerator
   D. liquidity preference
   E. the *demand-pull*

6. If people do not consume all their income and put the unspent amount into a bank or buy a security with it, in national income and product terms they are 6.___
   A. saving but not investing
   B. investing but not saving
   C. both saving and investing
   D. neither saving nor investing
   E. none of these

7. The *marginal propensity to consume* means the 7.___
   A. kinds of consumption goods that would be purchased if the family received extra income
   B. amount of income at which family consumption is just equal to family income
   C. average amount of each dollar of income spent on consumption
   D. ratio of extra consumption expenditure to extra income
   E. none of these

8. If Net National Product is rising, which of the following is MOST likely to occur without any discretionary policy decision being involved? 8.___
   A(n)
   A. decrease in government spending on goods and services
   B. decrease in social security payments to the aged
   C. increase in tax rates
   D. increase in tax receipts
   E. none of these

9. If the investment-interest curve is nearly vertical, then 9.___
   A. a small change in interest rates will have a substantial effect on the level of investment
   B. a tight money policy will be effective, but not an easy money policy
   C. it is very difficult to change Net National Product through monetary policy alone
   D. monetary policy will be effective in stimulating investment demand, but not in choking it off
   E. none of these

10. Assuming a required 20 percent reserve ratio, a small single large city bank which receives a net cash deposit of $1,000 is in a position to lend out an extra 10.___
    A. $5,000 B. $4,000 C. $1,000
    D. $800 E. none of these

11. The MAIN purpose of legal reserve requirements is to 11.___
    A. make the public's deposits safe and liquid
    B. keep the commercial banks from becoming too profitable
    C. enable the Federal Reserve authorities to control the amount of demand deposits that the Member Banks can create
    D. prevent *bank runs*
    E. none of these

12. A *favorable balance of trade* in a country which is at full employment tends directly to 12.___
   A. raise the level of real income
   B. raise the level of real consumption
   C. reduce inflationary pressures
   D. produce inflationary pressures
   E. none of these

13. A so-called *scientific tariff* which equalizes the cost of all production at home and abroad will 13.___
   A. avoid foreigners' complaints about being unfairly shut out of our market
   B. reduce both imports and exports virtually to zero
   C. force foreign producers to raise their wage levels
   D. assure us the benefits of comparative advantage
   E. none of these

14. Capital formation in underdeveloped areas is NOT made difficult because of 14.___
   A. low incomes
   B. the desire to emulate foreign consumption standards
   C. difficulties in borrowing abroad
   D. the bourgeois ethic stressing frugality and acquisitiveness and the consequent virtue of thrift
   E. none of these

15. Which of the following is NOT among the four factors which certain economists consider MOST important in promoting economic development? 15.___
   A. Productivity
   B. Natural resources
   C. Capital formation
   D. Technology
   E. None of these

16. Which of the following is NOT among the measures which certain economists urge for the development of industry? 16.___
   A. Established price control as a check against inflation
   B. Raising tariffs to promote industry
   C. Creating a surplus to finance capital formation
   D. Reforming the tax structure to finance *social overhead capital*
   E. None of these

17. The percentage of the world's population living in areas which are classified as underdeveloped is 17.___
   A. one-third
   B. one-half
   C. two-thirds
   D. three-quarters
   E. none of these

18. The optimum economic situation in regard to population in any country is 18.___
   A. that number of people whose labor will produce the largest possible per capita product
   B. the greatest number of people that country has ever had
   C. that time in a country's history of population where there has been developed the highest per capita income

D. one in which there is a balance between industrial and agricultural workers
E. none of these

19. Our rational objectives in the development of backward areas would be based on the 19.___
A. desire to import from them goods that they can produce more advantageously than we can at home
B. need to extend markets as an outlet for our exports so that we can avoid slumps
C. need to offset the appeals of communism in those areas
D. altruistic and ethical desire to create a more free and humane world society
E. none of these

20. Secular stagnation, according to Alvin Hansen, was NOT to be accounted for by 20.___
A. slowing population increase
B. competition with low-wage foreign labor
C. high corporate saving
D. passing of the frontier's free land
E. bias towards capital-saving invention

21. In teaching the forms of business organization, which of the following terms would the teacher be LEAST likely to explain? 21.___
A. Limited liability
B. Absentee ownership
C. Equity capital
D. Reserve ratio
E. None of these

22. The statement that imperfect competition prevails in a given industry means that prices in that industry are determined 22.___
A. by government regulation
B. by a single firm with a monopoly position
C. solely by conditions in the market
D. by the competing firms' decisions
E. none of these

23. The tax in the United States which MOST closely meets the needs of a sound tax system is the _____ tax. 23.___
A. personal
B. excess profits
C. death and inheritance
D. excise
E. none of these

24. In teaching the topic of exchange, a point of emphasis would be the fact that at least nine-tenths of all transactions (in terms of value) are accomplished by the use of 24.___
A. Federal Reserve notes
B. promissory notes
C. checks
D. bills of exchange
E. none of these

25. The United States Government prefers to sell defense bonds to individuals rather than to banks because the 25.___
   A. average person hoards his high wages in times of prosperity
   B. banks are reluctant to invest large sums of money in such bonds
   C. tendency of such sales is to avert inflation
   D. administration fears the domination of the Government by banking interests
   E. none of these

KEY (CORRECT ANSWERS)

1. C
2. C
3. C
4. E
5. A

6. A
7. D
8. D
9. C
10. B

11. C
12. D
13. B
14. D
15. A

16. A
17. C
18. A
19. D
20. B

21. D
22. D
23. A
24. C
25. C

TEST 4

DIRECTIONS: Each question or incomplete statement is followed by several suggested answers or completions. Select the one that BEST answers the question or completes the statement. *PRINT THE LETTER OF THE CORRECT ANSWER IN THE SPACE AT THE RIGHT.*

1. Economics is a social science because 1.___
   A. tables and graphs are used
   B. theory and empirical evidence are related
   C. the scientific method is applied to human behavior
   D. it deals with the allocation of scarce resources to material ends
   E. none of the above

2. The factors of production are USUALLY considered to be 2.___
   I. technology II. land III. labor
   IV. climate V. capital

   The CORRECT answer is:
   A. II, III, IV B. III, IV, V C. I, II, III
   D. II, III, V E. I, IV, V

3. Division of labor is USUALLY defined as 3.___
   A. everyone doing the same amount of work
   B. communism
   C. specialization
   D. none of the above
   E. all of the above

4. Economizing is necessary because 4.___
   A. there is not enough money for everybody
   B. resources are scarce in relation to human desires
   C. it is immoral for things to be wasted
   D. all of the above
   E. none of the above

5. The economist needs to know 5.___
   A. only mathematics because economics deals only with quantities
   B. mainly economic theory because economic behavior is common sense
   C. mainly the development of economic thought and institutions
   D. a minimum about human behavior plus economics
   E. as much as possible about the universe including, especially, economics and statistics

6. Free economic goods are those 6.___
   A. which are not important
   B. given to us by our parents
   C. given to us by the government
   D. given to us by nature and requiring no effort to make usable
   E. none of the above

7. The law of diminishing returns means that 7.___
   A. the more people work, the less is produced
   B. if one factor of production increases more slowly, eventually there will be a decline in productivity
   C. as population increases geometrically, food production increases arithmetically
   D. as labor increases, production per person declines
   E. all of the above

8. Living standards depend upon the 8.___
   A. number of people in an area
   B. ability to produce commodities
   C. ability to utilize commodities
   D. none of the above
   E. all of the above

9. The industrial revolution 9.___
   I. had nothing to do with world population increase
   II. did not develop where slavery was the basis of the economy
   III. has not influenced most of the people of the world
   IV. developed first in Britain and spread east and west
   V. all of the above

   The CORRECT answer is:
   A. I, III B. I, II C. II, III
   D. II, IV E. V

10. World population has increased because 10.___
   A. the birth rate has risen sharply
   B. the death rate has fallen sharply
   C. people are not practicing birth control
   D. all of the above
   E. none of the above

11. The amount of natural resources is 11.___
   I. fixed and unchanging
   II. dependent upon the level of technology
   III. subject to periodic fluctuations
   IV. subject to depletion
   V. all of the above

   The CORRECT answer is:
   A. I, II B. I, III C. II, III
   D. II, IV E. V

12. The accumulation of capital in an economy means the 12.___
   A. amount of money that is saved
   B. growth of output capacity
   C. rise in values on the stock market
   D. none of the above
   E. all of the above

13. The efficiency of production depends upon 13.___
    A. the division of labor and exchange
    B. mass production and mechanization
    C. automation and cybernetics
    D. none of the above
    E. all of the above

14. To increase output, we must do the following: 14.___
    I. increase hours of work
    II. increase the labor force
    III. increase output capacity
    IV. increase leisure time
    V. none of the above

    The CORRECT answer is:
    A. I, II, III B. I, II, IV C. I, III, IV
    D. II, III, IV E. V

15. Our economic system transforms competition into cooperation by 15.___
    A. freedom of contract
    B. intervention of the government
    C. operation of the price system in commodity markets
    D. all of the above
    E. none of the above

16. Arrange the following great economic thinkers chronologically: 16.___
    I. John Maynard Keynes II. Adam Smith
    III. Karl Marx IV. David Ricardo
    V. Thorstein Veblen

    The CORRECT answer is:
    A. II, III, IV, I, V B. II, IV, III, V, I
    C. II, III, IV, V, I D. IV, II, III, I, V
    E. IV, II, III, V, I

17. The price system tells businessmen how much of what to produce if 17.___
    A. workable competition exists in the market
    B. consumers buy on the basis of advertising only
    C. income is equally distributed only
    D. all of the above
    E. none of the above

18. Place these stages of economic development in sequence from the earliest to the latest: 18.___
    I. Machine technology and industrial capitalism
    II. Hunting and food-gathering
    III. Plow-agriculture and irrigation
    IV. Pastoralism and digging-stick agriculture
    V. Commercial capitalism

    The CORRECT answer is:
    A. II, III, IV, I, V B. II, III, IV, V, I
    C. II, IV, III, V, I D. IV, II, III, I, V
    E. IV, II, III, V, I

19. Modern industrial society is based PRIMARILY upon the following: 19.___
I. Forests II. Coal III. Gold
IV. Iron ore V. Petroleum

The CORRECT answer is:
A. I, II, III B. II, IV, V C. I, III, IV
D. I, III, V E. II, III, IV

20. Inequality of income is needed in an economy 20.___
I. to create an aristocracy of wealth
II. to make savings available for investment
III. to persuade people to work harder
IV. all of the above
V. none of the above

The CORRECT answer is:
A. I, II B. I, III C. IV
D. V E. II, III

21. Limitations upon freedom of occupational choice in the United States include 21.___
A. inequality of income distribution
B. discrimination in employment
C. inequality of educational or training opportunities
D. inadequate vocational guidance and apprentice training
E. all of the above

22. The concept of equilibrium involves the idea that 22.___
A. the economy can operate with no fluctuations
B. fluctuations tend to be self-correcting
C. there must be perfect competition for it to work
D. none of the above
E. all of the above

23. An economic theory is scientific 23.___
I. even if it requires many assumptions and has no relation to the actual operation of the economy
II. if it is consistent, even if it has little value for forecasting
III. if it is internally consistent and has a minimum of assumptions
IV. if it has considerable usefulness in forecasting
V. all of the above

The CORRECT answer is:
A. I, II B. I, III C. II, III
D. III, IV E. V

24. The fallacy of composition indicates that 24.___
A. if one event follows another, it is caused by it
B. if someone acts as we would, the action is correct
C. a knowledge of economics is needed to see economic contradictions
D. actions of individuals in their own self-interest may lead to results in the aggregate which injure their interest
E. none of the above

25. Gross national product is the 25.___
A. entire wealth of a country
B. entire production less depreciation
C. value of the annual output of all commodities
D. income of all wage and salary earners

KEY (CORRECT ANSWERS)

1. C
2. D
3. C
4. B
5. E

6. D
7. B
8. E
9. D
10. B

11. D
12. B
13. E
14. A
15. D

16. B
17. A
18. C
19. B
20. E

21. E
22. B
23. D
24. D
25. C

TEST 5

DIRECTIONS: Each question or incomplete statement is followed by several suggested answers or completions. Select the one that BEST answers the question or completes the statement. *PRINT THE LETTER OF THE CORRECT ANSWER IN THE SPACE AT THE RIGHT.*

1. National income consists of the 1.___
   A. value of goods and services from the private and government sectors of the economy
   B. income of all factors of production during a year
   C. income that is available to consumers annually
   D. income that producers receive after savings
   E. none of the above

2. Net investment can be defined as 2.___
   I. the amount of capital goods added to output capacity annually
   II. the amount of stocks and bonds purchased in one year
   III. gross investment minus depreciation
   IV. none of the above
   V. all of the above

   The CORRECT answer is:
   A. I, II B. I, III C. II, III
   D. IV E. V

3. As the United States economy developed after the Civil War, 3.___
   A. the merger movement among business firms increased
   B. industry began to become more important than agriculture
   C. broader markets led to greater specialization and mass production
   D. industrial capitalists and financiers became more dominant
   E. all of the above

4. Gross national product was 4.___
   A. smaller in 1929 than 1932
   B. smaller in 1939 than 1929
   C. larger in 1939 than 1945
   D. none of the above
   E. all of the above

5. The impact of technology upon the economy would follow which sequence according to Schumpeter: 5.___
   I. Innovation
   II. Acceptance of innovation
   III. Invention
   IV. Scientific development
   V. Financing

   The CORRECT answer is:
   A. I, II, V, IV, III
   B. IV, III, I, V, II
   C. IV, I, III, V, II
   D. III, IV, V, I, II
   E. II, IV, III, I, V

6. If productivity grows more rapidly than production, 6.___
   A. we may have growing inflation
   B. we may have growing unemployment
   C. we may need more unskilled labor
   D. a larger part of the labor force may be needed in manufacturing
   E. none of the above

7. Inflation means that 7.___
   I. the income of stockholders will decline
   II. there is a general rise in the value of money
   III. there is a general rise in the prices of commodities
   IV. the weighted index of wholesale prices rises
   V. the index of physical output rises

   The CORRECT answer is:
   A. I, II B. I, III C. II, III
   D. III, IV E. I, V

8. The advantage of a weighted price index over one that is not weighted consists of the fact that the 8.___
   A. weighted index is easier to calculate
   B. data for the unweighted index is harder to find
   C. unweighted index is more complex
   D. unweighted index does not reflect the importance of the component commodities
   E. all of the above

9. The PRINCIPAL forms of specialization today are by 9.___
   I. income II. vocation III. age
   IV. task V. geography

   The CORRECT answer is:
   A. I, II, III B. I, III, IV C. I, III, V
   D. II, III, IV E. II, IV, V

10. As the level of prices changes, 10.___
    A. it has the same effects on all consumers and producers
    B. the value of money varies inversely with these changes
    C. the value of commodities remains in unvarying relationship to each other
    D. none of the above
    E. all of the above

11. The effect of inflationary policies upon the economy depends on the 11.___
    A. percentage of unemployment
    B. balance of international payments
    C. marginal propensity to save
    D. none of the above
    E. all of the above

12. A policy of inflation is necessary to 12.___
I. increase the purchasing power of the dollar
II. increase living standards
III. pay off the national debt
IV. prevent overexpansion at full employment
V. all of the above

The CORRECT answer is:
A. I, II B. I, III C. I, IV
D. II, III E. V

13. Private property rights are becoming increasingly limited because 13.___
A. specialization is making people more interdependent
B. the role of the government in the economy is greater
C. the density of population is rising
D. stock ownership has become divorced from control
E. all of the above

14. The profit motive is 14.___
I. the only incentive businessmen have in the modern economy
II. a manifestation of the spirit of acquisitiveness
III. transforms private greed into public benefit through competition
IV. the only motive making people work under private capitalism
V. responsible for all economic development

The CORRECT answer is:
A. I, II B. I, III C. I, IV
D. II, III E. IV, V

15. Price competition exists when 15.___
A. there is a large number of independent buyers and sellers
B. the commodities are comparable
C. both buyers and sellers have reasonable knowledge about the commodities
D. there is freedom of entry into the market
E. all of the above

16. Money replaced barter because 16.___
I. as specialization increased trade expanded
II. as trade expanded barter became too time consuming
III. people desired precious metals more than other commodities
IV. the increasing division of labor made commodity payment increasingly difficult
V. none of the above

The CORRECT answer is:
A. I, II B. I, III C. II, III
D. II, IV E. V

17. Commercial banks are 17.___
   A. reservoirs for peoples' savings
   B. creators of most of the money in use
   C. not regulated by any one
   D. in control of interest rates
   E. playing a growing role in the market for corporation bonds

18. Excess reserves are 18.___
   I. the excess of deposits over loans
   II. those over legal reserve requirements
   III. loanable funds
   IV. none of the above
   V. all of the above

   The CORRECT answer is:
   A. I, II B. I, III C. II, III
   D. IV E. V

19. The Federal Reserve system can control the volume of check money 19.___
   A. by open market operations in government bonds
   B. changing the rediscount rate
   C. altering reserve requirements
   D. none of the above
   E. all of the above

20. The velocity of circulation of money has 20.___
   A. nothing to do with the volume of money
   B. been subject to large short-term fluctuations
   C. been subject to large long-term fluctuations
   D. all of the above
   E. none of the above

21. Effective demand for goods and services is 21.___
   A. determined by the funds spent for consumption and investment
   B. disposable personal income
   C. the proportion of national income saved
   D. corporation expenditure for expansion
   E. all of the above

22. As income for the consumer rises, 22.___
   A. consumption rises as rapidly
   B. savings increases more slowly
   C. consumption rises more rapidly
   D. savings rises more rapidly
   E. none of the above

23. Businessmen invest when 23.___
   A. they want to increase their firm's efficiency
   B. expected profits are larger than the going interest rate
   C. demand for their commodity exceeds their output capacity
   D. none of the above
   E. all of the above

24. Money consists of 24.___
I. legal tender only
II. generally acceptable symbols of claims upon commodities
III. only gold and silver
IV. a medium of exchange and measure of value
V. currency but not checks

The CORRECT answer is:
A. I, III B. I, V C. II, IV
D. III, V E. I, IV

25. Pre-Keynsian thinking among most economists considered that full employment was the rule because 25.___
I. according to Say's law, *supply creates its own demand*
II. prices and wages were becoming less flexible
III. the interest rate in a free market tends to equalize saving and investment
IV. barriers to trade were growing after World War I
V. none of the above

The CORRECT answer is:
A. I, III B. I, II C. II, IV
D. II, III E. V

KEY (CORRECT ANSWERS)

1. B
2. B
3. E
4. D
5. B

6. B
7. D
8. D
9. E
10. B

11. E
12. C
13. E
14. D
15. E

16. D
17. B
18. C
19. E
20. B

21. A
22. D
23. E
24. C
25. A

EXAMINATION SECTION

TEST 1

DIRECTIONS: Each question or incomplete statement is followed by several suggested answers or completions. Select the one that BEST answers the question or completes the statement. *PRINT THE LETTER OF THE CORRECT ANSWER IN THE SPACE AT THE RIGHT.*

1. Of the following, the result MOST likely to be produced by international cartels is 1.___
   A. more competition among small businesses
   B. better trade opportunities for all business
   C. more employment
   D. higher prices for consumer goods
   E. fairer sharing of world trade and profits

2. Adam Smith in THE WEALTH OF NATIONS advocates that nations should 2.___
   A. try to accumulate gold and silver
   B. follow a policy of free trade
   C. practice the mercantile theory of trade
   D. build up colonial empires
   E. increase government regulation of industry and trade

3. Which of the following is *likely* to be MOST conducive to a long-range increase in real wages? 3.___
   A. A reduction in the number of large corporations
   B. A reduction in the rate of capital investment
   C. Technological improvements
   D. High protective tariffs
   E. An increase in the volume of credit and currency

4. Which of the following *normally* occurs when a commercial bank makes a loan to a business firm? The bank's liabilities 4.___
   A. and assets *increase*
   B. and assets *decrease*
   C. and assets are *unaffected*
   D. *increase* and its assets *decrease*
   E. *decrease* and its assets *increase*

5. A truly *laissez-faire* economic system came CLOSEST to existing in 5.___
   A. Europe in the Middle Ages
   B. Great Britain in the eighteenth century
   C. Great Britain and the United States in the nineteenth century
   D. the United States in the twentieth century
   E. France and Germany in the nineteenth century

6. Which one of the following economic policies is NOT consistent with the other four? 6.___
   A. Decrease of the rediscount rates by the Federal Reserve Banks
   B. Government appropriations under the European Recovery Program
   C. Increase in individual income taxes
   D. Increase in open-market buying operations by the Federal Reserve Banks
   E. Increase in time permitted for paying installment buying obligations

7. The PRIMARY function of legal reserve requirements of the Federal Reserve Board today is to 7.___
   A. protect depositors from asset depreciation
   B. provide commercial banks with liquidity
   C. force commercial banks to lend money to the Federal Reserve System
   D. encourage commercial banks to save part of their deposits
   E. allow the central bank to control the creation of money

8. Which of the following BEST describes the relationship between the United States balance-of-payments deficit and the persistence of relatively high unemployment levels in the United States? 8.___
   A. The balance-of-payments deficit caused the unemployment.
   B. The low level of employment caused the deficit.
   C. The excess of imports over exports caused the deficit and the low level of economic activity.
   D. The tools which the United States could use to mitigate unemployment might aggravate the deficit.
   E. Inflation in the United States caused both the deficit and the unemployment.

9. An immediate economic consequence of the reunification of Germany was 9.___
   A. a dramatic increase in interest rates in general and unemployment in East Germany
   B. devaluation of the mark
   C. a decrease in the DAX stock market index
   D. restructuring of the Bundesbank

10. All of the following are examples of regional economic integrative organizations EXCEPT the 10.___
   A. Central American Common Market
   B. Caribbean Free Trade Association
   C. Andean Group
   D. Organization of American States
   E. European Free Trade Association

11. The total of the entries on the credit side of a nation's balance of payments must equal the total of those on the debit side. Yet, one often hears of a nation's deficit or surplus in the balance of payments. 11.___
The apparent paradox is resolved when one realizes that
   A. not all international transactions are reported to the authorities responsible for collecting balance-of-payments statistics
   B. balance-of-payments statistics are notoriously inaccurate
   C. all the foreign aid receipts or payments are not included when measuring payments imbalances
   D. entries, such as changes in monetary reserves, considered as compensatory transactions, are not included when measuring payments imbalances
   E. the terms "deficit" and "surplus" are actually totally unrelated to the balance of payments

12. Of the following, the statement which describes MOST accurately the operation of stock exchanges under the Securities Exchange Act is that 12.___
   A. all securities and stock exchanges are required to be registered with a regulatory agency of the state in which they are located
   B. control of credit for speculative purposes is maintained by the Federal Reserve System rather than the Securities and Exchange Commission itself
   C. by controlling stock sales, the speculative aspects of securities purchasing have all but been eliminated by the Securities and Exchange Commission
   D. control of stock exchange operations is restricted to pegging of security prices
   E. use of publicity concerning securities is the primary method of maintaining fair practices and protecting the investor

13. Much of the economic theory associated with the name of John Maynard Keynes was occasioned by the 13.___
   A. fact that many people spend money almost solely to impress their associates
   B. development of labor unions in England
   C. rapid growth of the population of the earth
   D. development of oligopoly in the United States
   E. worldwide depression of the 1930's

14. All of the following have written significant works on economic problems in the United States EXCEPT 14.___
   A. Edward Bellamy
   B. Stuart Chase
   C. Henry George
   D. Upton Sinclair
   E. Lorado Taft

15. All of the following are arguments for reciprocal trade agreements EXCEPT the argument that they 15.___
   A. encourage economic nationalism
   B. foster economic peace and stability

C. promote scientific methods of dealing with trade problems
D. make countries interdependent
E. tend to encourage countries to produce goods for which they are best adapted

Questions 16-25.

DIRECTIONS: In questions 16 to 25, select the alternatives that most satisfactorily complete the statements or answer the questions, basing your choice on information given in the chart which follows or on *your understanding of the economic history of the United States*.

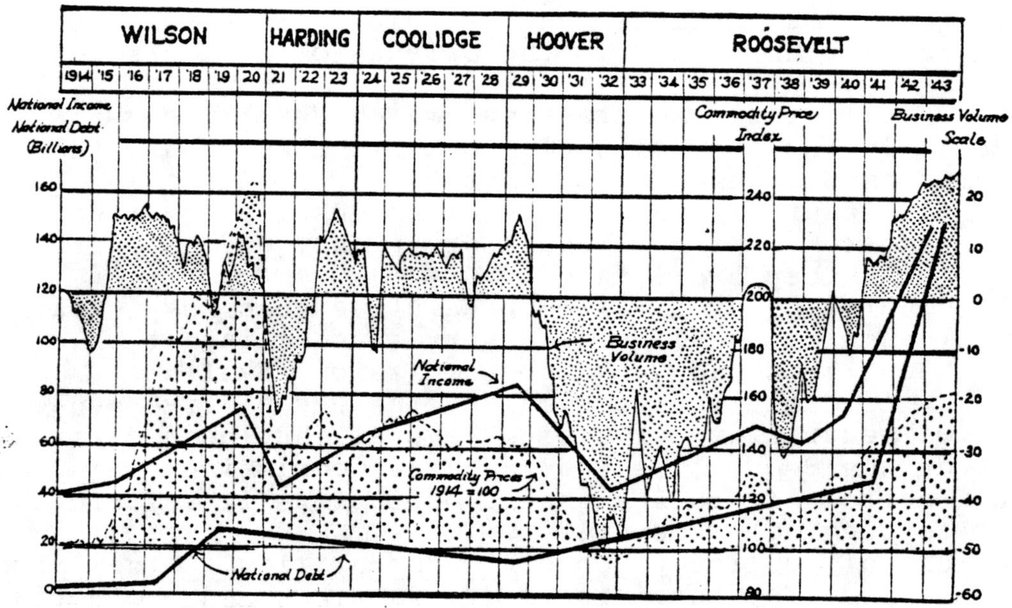

16. As used in the chart, the term *national debt* means the total amount owed by 16.____
   A. the United States Government to other nations
   B. the federal government
   C. the federal and state governments to United States citizens
   D. the United States Government and United States citizens to foreign persons or nations
   E. United States citizens to other nations

17. Which of the following statements about the national debt of the United States are TRUE? 17.____
   I. It increased sharply during both World Wars.
   II. It increased throughout the great depression.
   III. It decreased a third between World War I and the stock market crash.
   IV. In 1943, it had reached the highest point up to that time.

The CORRECT answer is:
A. I, II
B. I, III
C. I, IV
D. III, IV
E. All of the above

18. As used in the chart, the term *national income* means the 18.___
A. total of the incomes subject to the federal income tax
B. value of the goods produced and services rendered in the United States
C. value of goods and services exported
D. total of all government revenues in the United States
E. total revenues of the federal government from taxes and borrowing

19. Which of the following statements about the national income of the United States are TRUE? It 19.___
I. reached its highest point in the period between the declaration of World War I and the declaration of World War II
II. increased constantly after Franklin D. Roosevelt became President
III. increased more in Republican than in Democratic administrations

The CORRECT answer is:
A. None of the above
B. I *only*
C. I, II
D. I, III
E. II, III

20. The cost of living 20.___
A. depends exclusively upon the demand for and the supply of goods
B. is computed for this chart on the basis of the price level of 1937
C. is higher in depressions than in normal times
D. varies inversely with the purchasing power of money
E. normally decreases when the amount of money in circulation increases

21. As shown by the chart, the index of the cost of living in the United States 21.___
I. is based upon commodity prices in 1914
II. rose at approximately the same rate in both wars
III. remained fairly constant throughout the administrations of Harding and Coolidge
IV. reached a maximum of 165 during World War I

The CORRECT answer is:
A. I, II
B. I, III
C. I, IV
D. II, III
E. II, IV

22. The volume of business 22.___
A. is dependent upon the political party in power
B. reflects changes in the national debt
C. is measured by various indexes or "business barometers"
D. has little relation to prosperity and depression
E. depends chiefly upon the current tariff policy

23. Which of the following statements about the volume of business in the United States are TRUE? 23.___
I. It has fluctuated widely in the period covered by the chart.
II. It has shown the same general trends as the national income.
III. In the period shown, it has been both highest and lowest under Republican Presidents.
IV. It tends to increase in wartime.

The CORRECT answer is:
A. I, II, III
B. I, II, IV
C. I, III, IV
D. II, III, IV
E. All of the above

24. Temporary fluctuations in the value of money depend primarily on the 24.___
A. cost of food
B. backing for the money
C. national income
D. volume of business in the country
E. relation between the amount of money and credit and the volume of business

25. In the period shown, which of the following statements about the value of money in the United States are TRUE? It 25.___
I. was the greatest at the end of 1932
II. has shown an upward trend during the New Deal
III. rose sharply with the adoption of the Federal Reserve System
IV. remained higher in the present war than in World War I

The CORRECT answer is:
A. I, II
B. I, IV
C. II, III
D. II, IV
E. III, IV

KEY (CORRECT ANSWERS)

1. D
2. B
3. C
4. A
5. C
6. C
7. E
8. D
9. A
10. D
11. D
12. B
13. E
14. E
15. A
16. B
17. E
18. B
19. A
20. D
21. B
22. C
23. B
24. E
25. B

TEST 2

DIRECTIONS: Each question or incomplete statement is followed by several suggested answers or completions. Select the one that BEST answers the question or completes the statement. *PRINT THE LETTER OF THE CORRECT ANSWER IN THE SPACE AT THE RIGHT.*

1. Which one of the following would be included in calculating gross national product? 1.___
   A. Housework done by wife
   B. Indirect business taxes
   C. Social security payments
   D. Farm subsidies

2. Of the following, which one will tend to cause an outflow of gold from the United States? 2.___
   A. Deflation
   B. Balanced budgets
   C. Inflation
   D. Increased rediscount rates

3. Which one of the statements below would Keynes have used to explain how short-term declines in business cycles occur? 3.___
   A. The interaction of the accelerator and multiplier provides the leverage action.
   B. The marginal propensity to consume declines as income rises.
   C. The marginal propensity to consume rises as incomes decline and the leverage works in reverse.
   D. Multipliers and accelerators operate more on consumer than on durable goods.

4. Which one of the following pairs of factors tends to distort the Net National Product as a reliable economic indicator? 4.___
   A. Inflation and population growth
   B. Hours of labor and social security payments
   C. Exports and imports
   D. Taxes and current capital consumption

5. Which one of the following has the same effect as an import on the American balance of payments? 5.___
   A. An American receiving dividend payments on an investment in Venezuelan oil
   B. An American taking a Swissair plane from Paris to Zurich
   C. Goods shipped from Paris to New York in an American vessel
   D. A foreign student at Harvard receiving a stipend from his parents in Brazil

6. Which one of the following does NOT hamper the effectiveness of a monetary policy as a countercyclical weapon? 6.___
   A. Prediction and timing
   B. Recurrent United States Treasury borrowing
   C. Control over margin requirements
   D. Large bank holdings of federal securities

7. Which of the following would have to be increased if a commercial bank is to be able to expand its credit? 7.___
   A. Legal reserves
   B. Rediscount rates
   C. Purchase of securities by the Open Market Committee
   D. Public sale of United States Treasury bonds

8. Which one of the following is an inflationary factor in periods of full employment? 8.___
   A. Budgetary surpluses
   B. Tax increases
   C. Sale of government securities by the Federal Reserve Open Market Committee
   D. Budgetary deficits

9. Which one of the following was the PRIMARY reason for the United States going off the gold standard in 1934? To 9.___
   A. increase the nation's gold reserves
   B. break the power of Wall Street bankers
   C. bring about a rise in prices
   D. satisfy demands of numismatic interests

10. The National Industrial Recovery Act of the New Deal sought to encourage economic recovery by 10.___
   A. permitting agreements limiting competition
   B. subsidizing price reductions
   C. granting liberal tax-exemption for new industries
   D. giving economic aid for small business

11. If the price of a commodity is 38 cents today and the index is 128, what was the APPROXIMATE price in the base year? 11.___
   A. $1.64 B. $.90 C. $.64 D. $.30

12. The concept of parity as employed in American agriculture means that 12.___
   A. farm income should remain stable over the business cycle
   B. a given output should always provide the farmer with the same real income
   C. the purchasing power of the farmer's dollar should remain constant
   D. the prices of farm commodities should remain stable

13. Which one of the following is likely to result in an oligopoly during a period of prosperity? 13.___
   A. Price leadership decline
   B. Differentiation of product
   C. Industry concentration ratios grow
   D. Development of monopsony

14. As of December, 1992, in which one of the following are data CORRECTLY matched with dimensions of our economic system? 14.___
   A. Gross National Product - $623 billion
   B. Size of American labor force - 42 million
   C. United States gold reserves - $15 billion
   D. National debt - over $3 trillion

15. Of the following, which one is MOST effective in stimulating our economy and achieving full employment? 15.___
   A. Balanced federal budgets
   B. Federal budgetary deficits financed by banks
   C. Tax reduction and curtailed federal spending
   D. The floating of federal bonds in a public sale to cover budgetary deficits

16. Which one of the following measures permits price arrangements which interfere with competitive market conditions the other three acts sought to maintain? 16.___
   A. Sherman Act
   B. Clayton Anti-trust Act
   C. McGuire Act
   D. Celler-Kefauver Act

17. Which of the following statements represent the thinking of Adam Smith? 17.___
   I. He favored state interference in wage contracts.
   II. He opposed grants of monopoly by the state.
   III. He favored free trade among nations.
   IV. He believed that the wealth of a nation depends on the amassing of bullion.

   The CORRECT answer is:
   A. I, IV
   B. I, III, IV
   C. II, III, IV
   D. II, III

18. Of the following, the PRINCIPAL objective of Reaganomics, the economic policy of the Reagan administration,was to 18.___
   A. cut federal taxes, reduce government spending, maintain control over the growth of money
   B. reduce the federal budget by eliminating revenue-sharing aid to cities and local governments, dismantling the departments of Energy and Education, ordering a 10-12% cut in spending by all non-military departments
   C. increase defense authorization levels while cutting aid to under-developed nations
   D. allow stock market prices to find their own levels, raise the interest rates for passbook savings accounts, encourage savers to invest in the All Savers Certificates

19. The MOST common barrier to economic progress in developing countries is a *shortage* of 19.___
   A. raw materials
   B. agricultural land
   C. capital
   D. unskilled workers

20. Of the following natural resources, the one of which the United States has the LARGEST reserve is 20.___
   A. coal
   B. gas
   C. iron
   D. petroleum

21. Of the following situations, the one which should be highlighted as a cause of inflation is 21.___
   A. low wages and a surplus of consumer goods
   B. a limited supply of money and an expanding population
   C. a high rate of employment and a shortage of consumer goods
   D. an increase in taxes and a decrease in government spending

22. The MAJOR source of United States Federal Government income today is the 22.___
   A. sales tax
   B. personal income tax
   C. corporate income tax
   D. social insurance tax and contributions

23. When interest rates drop, the *most likely* result is that 23.___
   A. borrowing for business expansion increases
   B. the rate of inflation increases
   C. unemployment increases
   D. the national growth speeds up

24. The new industrialism of 19th century England was defended, despite its exploitation of the working man, by the 24.___
   A. Classical School of economists as exemplified by Malthus and Ricardo
   B. Utopian Socialists like Fourier
   C. Tories under the leadership of Disraeli
   D. Marxist Socialists

25. The conclusion that economic forces alone determine the course of history is *most frequently* associated with 25.___
   A. Adam Smith
   B. Karl Marx
   C. Jean Jacques Rousseau
   D. Leo Tolstoi

KEY (CORRECT ANSWERS)

1. B
2. C
3. B
4. A
5. B

6. C
7. C
8. D
9. C
10. A

11. D
12. B
13. B
14. D
15. B

16. C
17. D
18. A
19. C
20. A

21. C
22. B
23. A
24. C
25. B

TEST 3

DIRECTIONS: Each question or incomplete statement is followed by several suggested answers or completions. Select the one that BEST answers the question or completes the statement. *PRINT THE LETTER OF THE CORRECT ANSWER IN THE SPACE AT THE RIGHT.*

1. Which one of the following would be MOST likely to have a limiting effect on the application of the Law of Monopoly Price? 1.___
   A. The producer's knowledge of consumer demand
   B. The producer's dissatisfaction with current profits
   C. The producer's experimentation with varied prices
   D. The producer's fear of potential competition

2. Which one of the following is NOT considered a cause of inflation by economists? 2.___
   A. The effects of "wage-push"
   B. The effects of "demand-pull"
   C. The effects of administered prices
   D. The effects of high taxes

3. Industries that produce hard goods are typically the hardest hit in a depression because 3.___
   A. the purchase of capital goods may be deferred but demand for consumer durables remains the same
   B. non-durable consumer goods depreciate more rapidly than capital goods
   C. the impact of a fall in consumer demand centers primarily on production and employment in these industries
   D. capital goods industries are industries of low concentration and are highly competitive

4. National income data for any series of years would show that 4.___
   A. "national income" fluctuates far more sharply than does "gross national product"
   B. "national income" always equals "gross national product" because the former is the money equivalent of the latter
   C. government payments to individuals, such as social security payments, are excluded from "personal income"
   D. conversion of current dollars into constant dollars is necessary for reliable generalizations concerning trends

5. One measure which the Federal Reserve authorities could take to combat deflation would be to 5.___
   A. purchase government securities on the open market
   B. raise the Member Bank reserve requirements
   C. increase margin requirements covering stock market purchases
   D. increase rediscount rates on commercial paper

6. The CHIEF function of bank reserve requirements is to 6.___
   A. limit the total volume of credit that a bank can extend
   B. prevent runs on banks
   C. serve as backing for Federal Reserve Notes
   D. eliminate the need for "time deposits"

7. When the parity price ratio is around 80, it means that 7.___
   A. prices received by farmers have not risen as much as have the prices they must pay
   B. prices paid by farmers have not risen as much as have the prices received by farmers
   C. the government has set a price support of 80% of parity
   D. farm incomes are fluctuating far less than non-farm incomes

8. Study of United States corporate financing practices during the period after World War II indicates more financing by 8.___
   A. bond issues than by stock issues, partly due to the tax advantage involved in bond financing
   B. stock issues than by bond issues, partly due to the tax advantage involved in stock financing
   C. stock issues than by bond issues, due to the shortage of equity capital
   D. bond issues than by stock issues, due to the shortage of equity capital

9. Which one of the following statements concerning the control of monetary and credit conditions in the United States is INCORRECT? 9.___
   A. The fact that the Federal Reserve Board supported the government securities market during World War II and after,resulted in member banks becoming independent of Federal Reserve restraints.
   B. The United States Treasury must work through the Federal Reserve System to effect its purposes in relation to money and credit supply.
   C. Since the early 1920's, the Federal Reserve authorities have relied chiefly on open-market operations rather than rediscount rate changes as the method of credit control.
   D. The policy of gold sterilization in the 1930's kept gold coming into the country from increasing the excess reserves then prevailing in the banks.

10. Which of the following concepts can be LEAST correctly associated with the economic theory of Alfred Marshall? 10.___
    A. "Economic man" B. Principle of continuity
    C. Representative firm D. Quasi-rent

11. John Bates Clark's MOST outstanding contribution to economic theory was in the field of 11.___
    A. public finance B. distribution
    C. imperfect competition D. institutional economics

12. Berle and Means found that the GREATEST number of corporations they surveyed were controlled by 12.___
   A. owners holding a majority of stock
   B. management, without special legal devices or material stock ownership
   C. special legal devices, including the issue of non-voting stock, voting trusts, and the like
   D. owners holding a minority of stock

13. Macroanalysis in economics centers attention upon 13.___
   A. mathematical statement of economic laws
   B. problems of an economy as a whole
   C. statistical approach to economic phenomena
   D. problems of pricing and marketing

14. The theory of opportunity costs is MOST closely related to 14.___
   A. risk factors in investment
   B. mobility of factors of production
   C. liquidity preferences
   D. time preferences

15. The problem of price determination under conditions of joint cost is MOST clearly the concern of a 15.___
   A. retail grocer
   B. department store entrepreneur
   C. real estate broker
   D. meat packer

16. Under which of the following circumstances will an employer's demand for labor NOT become more inelastic? 16.___
   A. As his marginal-receipts curve becomes more inelastic
   B. As the ratio of his labor costs to his total costs becomes greater
   C. As it becomes more difficult for him to substitute land or capital for labor
   D. As the supply of the other factors of production becomes more inelastic

17. Which of the following conditions may result from the existence of administered prices in our economy? 17.___
   I. A greater ease of adjustment for the flexible price industries
   II. Impairment of the adjustability of the economy
   III. Impairment of sales in other fields of enterprise
   IV. Unemployment in the administered price industries

   The CORRECT answer is:
   A. I, II, IV
   B. II, III, IV
   C. I, II, III
   D. I, III, IV

18. Which one of the following was TRUE of the American economy in the period 1946-1953? 18.___
   A. While the real income of most American workers increased, that of the farmers declined.
   B. This was a period of general price stability.
   C. The reconversion from war production to civilian production caused a depression immediately after World War II.
   D. On the whole, this was a period of labor-management peace.

19. Which one of the following is the largest single item in the annual balance-of-payments for the United States? 19.___
    A. Exports and imports of goods
    B. Expenses of American travelers abroad
    C. Capital exports from the United States
    D. Income from foreign investments

20. Which one of the following economic principles is CORRECT with regard to the demand for labor in a particular industry? 20.___
    A. The demand for labor has no relationship to the value of the product.
    B. The more elastic the demand for the product, the more inelastic is the demand for the labor required to produce it.
    C. The greater the proportion which the cost of labor bears to the total cost of the product, the more inelastic is the demand for labor.
    D. The demand for a given type of labor tends to be elastic if good, cheap substitutes for this type of labor are available.

21. Which one of the following writers differs MOST markedly in his theories on international trade from the other three? 21.___
    A. Matthew Carey
    B. Richard Cobden
    C. Friedrich List
    D. Simon Patten

22. Which pair of writers have written books challenging each other's economic theories? 22.___
    A. A.A. Berle, Jr. - Gardner C. Means
    B. G.D.H. Cole - Barbara Wootton
    C. Friedrich A. Hayek - Herman Finer
    D. John M. Keynes - Alvin H. Hansen

23. Which economist is paired INCORRECTLY with his field of specialization? 23.___
    A. Herbert Harris - Labor
    B. Simon Kuznets - Banking
    C. William Z. Ripley - Railroads
    D. Frank W. Taussig - Tariffs

24. Which one of the following was MOST unlike the other three in social outlook? 24.___
    A. Ray Stannard Baker
    B. Gustavus Myers
    C. Alton B. Parker
    D. John Spargo

25. A monthly publication of the President's Council of Economic Advisers which deals with major aspects of business life is 25.___
    A. ECONOMIC INDICATORS
    B. THE STATISTICAL ABSTRACT OF THE UNITED STATES
    C. SURVEY OF CURRENT BUSINESS
    D. WORLD ECONOMIC SURVEY

KEY (CORRECT ANSWERS)

1. D
2. D
3. C
4. D
5. A

6. A
7. A
8. A
9. B
10. A

11. B
12. B
13. B
14. B
15. D

16. B
17. B
18. A
19. A
20. D

21. B
22. C
23. B
24. C
25. A

TEST 4

DIRECTIONS: Each question or incomplete statement is followed by several suggested answers or completions. Select the one that BEST answers the question or completes the statement. *PRINT THE LETTER OF THE CORRECT ANSWER IN THE SPACE AT THE RIGHT.*

1. In which one of the following is the definition INCORRECTLY matched with the term it defines? 1.___
   A. Administered price - A price set by management for private enterprise or by government for a public utility
   B. Monopolistic competition - Existence of a substantial number of sellers of identical or closely interchangeable products
   C. Oligopoly - A single seller of a product without a close substitute such as the local water company
   D. Monopsony - Pure monopoly on the buyer's side, such as the one employer of labor in an isolated mill town

2. Which one of the following represents the NEAREST approach to perfect competition? 2.___
   A. Differentiated products B. Oligopoly
   C. The stock market D. Monopolistic competition

3. Which one of the following is NOT a factor causing inflation? 3.___
   A. Excess spending beyond the supply of goods available for current purchase
   B. Costs and selling prices pushed up by strong labor unions while unemployment still exists
   C. Administered prices which set up rigidities in the price structure
   D. A budgetary surplus with tax receipts greater than expenditures

4. The term "double taxation" as applied to a corporation's income means that 4.___
   A. the corporation pays both an income tax and an excess profits tax
   B. some corporations pay excise taxes as well as income taxes
   C. a second tax is levied on income not distributed as dividends
   D. a tax is levied on both corporate income and the dividends paid the stockholders

5. Economists are generally agreed that 5.___
   A. government deficits have a depressing effect on total spending
   B. government budget policy can play an important role in stabilizing our American economy

C. a budgetary surplus tends to expand total spending
D. the size of the budgetary deficit or surplus has no appreciable effect on either total spending or economic activity

6. In order for a program of crop reduction in a specific crop to result in higher total revenue for a farmer growing that crop, the demand for that crop must be 6.___
A. proportional B. marginal
C. inelastic D. elastic

7. With the general abandonment of some of the basic requisites of the traditional gold standard, the par value for each of the monetary units of the world 7.___
A. no longer exists
B. is adjusted unilaterally by countries in the light of their balance of payments position
C. is adjusted through the International Monetary Fund
D. is regulated by regional agreements such as the European Payments Union

8. The "principle of comparative advantage" would be MOST closely related to a study of 8.___
A. the factors of production
B. specialization of labor
C. international trade
D. investment policies

9. The basic assumptions underlying the doctrines of laissez-faire and natural rights are also the basic assumptions underlying the 9.___
A. divine right theory and natural law
B. mercantile theory and divine right theory
C. social contract theory and natural law
D. social contract theory and state socialism

10. Which one of the following applies BOTH to preferred stocks and to bonds? 10.___
A. They receive payment only in case the corporation has made a profit.
B. They both enjoy a fixed rate of return.
C. Neither one receives any preferential treatment in case of bankruptcy.
D. Holders of both types of securities are part owners of the corporation.

11. To which one of the following can a nation resort in order to obtain a favorable balance of trade? 11.___
A. Increase the tariff on imports
B. Pass a law setting higher import quotas
C. Depreciate its currency
D. Borrow money from a creditor nation

12. As the amount of disposable personal income increases, there is a tendency to save more money than the opportunities for profitable investment can absorb. This statement is in accord with the theory of capital accumulation attributed to 12.___

A. John Maurice Clark B. John Maynard Keynes
C. Alfred Marshall D. Thorstein Veblen

13. Overhead costs are significant in our economy in that 13.___
   I. they introduce elements of immobility which may prevent the adjustment of production to demand
   II. when demand slackens, they force producers into fields with greater profit prospects
   III. they sometimes encourage cut-throat competition
   IV. the cut-throat competition engendered by overhead costs forces the least efficient firms out of business

   The CORRECT answer is:
   A. I, III B. I, III, IV
   C. II, IV D. III, IV

14. Which one of the following would be MOST likely to occur in perfect rather than imperfect competition? 14.___
   A. Oligopoly
   B. Price leadership
   C. Product differentiation
   D. Free mobility of factors of production

15. Economists who believe in the equilibrium theory of unemployment would be LEAST likely to place a major share of blame for unemployment on 15.___
   A. monetary conditions
   B. maldistribution of economic resources
   C. lack of mobility of labor
   D. government floors under prices and wages

16. Which one of the social functions listed below do interest and land rent perform? 16.___
   A. They act to withdraw resources from use in present consumption.
   B. They serve to direct their respective factors of production into the most valuable and useful channels.
   C. They stimulate increased supply of their respective factors.
   D. They help to maintain balance between the provision for present and future wants.

17. Review of interest rates in specific countries over long periods of time reveals long-term trends of 17.___
   A. constancy, that can most reasonably be explained in terms of persistent traits of human psychology
   B. variability, that can be most correctly associated with changes in the productivity of capital
   C. variability, that can be most correctly associated with cyclical fluctuations in the economy
   D. constancy, that can most reasonably be explained in terms of consistent superiority of capitalistic methods of production over the techniques of less developed economies

18. Which of the following are CORRECT statements of modern economic theory as related to profit? 18.___
  I. Pure profit tends to disappear as a state of balanced competition is approached.
  II. Pure profit results from the imperfections of competition.
  III. Pure profit is the net income of a business as a whole, rather than the return for entrepreneurial service.
  IV. Scientific management and insurance have minimized the validity of the concept of profit as "compensation for risk-taking."

  The CORRECT answer is:
  A. I, II, III, IV
  B. I, II
  C. III, IV
  D. I, III

19. A basic difference between the Brookings Institution and the National Bureau of Economic Research is that 19.___
  A. Brookings studies offer conclusions concerning policy, while the National Bureau tends to confine its studies to assembling and analyzing data
  B. the studies of the National Bureau offer conclusions concerning policy, while Brookings tends to confine its studies to assembling and analyzing data
  C. as an agency of the Federal government, the studies of the National Bureau are concerned primarily with fiscal policy
  D. Wesley C. Mitchell's long association with Brookings has tended to center its interest on problems of business cycles

20. Which two of the following theories of wages are MOST similar in their basic approach to the problem? 20.___
  I. Francis A. Walker - residual claimant theory
  II. F.W. Taussig - discounted marginal productivity theory
  III. John Davidson - bargaining theory
  IV. Karl Marx - exploitation theory

  The CORRECT answer is:
  A. I, II B. II, III C. III, IV D. I, IV

21. Which of the following is author of a book that develops the theoretical aspects of corporate activity? 21.___
  A. N.S. Buchanan
  B. A.A. Berle
  C. W.Z. Ripley
  D. J.T. Flynn

22. The standard twentieth century work on which much of the study of incidence and shifting of taxes has since been based,was written by 22.___
  A. Harold M. Groves
  B. Edwin R.A. Seligman
  C. William H. Steiner
  D. Hartley L. Lutz

23. Theoretical justification for social security legislation can be found in the theory of the causes of unemployment as stated by 23.___
I. A.H. Hansen
II. J.M. Keynes
III. J.B. Say
IV. Alfred Marshall

The CORRECT answer is:
A. I, II, III
B. III, IV
C. II, III
D. I, II

24. The Henry George theory of the Single Tax is based on which of the following concepts? 24.___
I. The Ricardian law of land rent
II. That a real estate owner must be taxed for all improvements he makes on the land
III. That land rent is the only source of unearned income
IV. That the Single Tax would force every landowner to put his land to the most productive use

The CORRECT answer is:
A. I, II, III
B. II, IV
C. I, III, IV
D. I, II, III, IV

25. Which one of the following did NOT influence the restatement of economic theory developed by John Stuart Mill? 25.___
A. Jeremy Bentham
B. Nassau William Senior
C. Saint-Simon
D. Carl Menger

KEY (CORRECT ANSWERS)

1. C
2. C
3. D
4. D
5. B

6. C
7. C
8. C
9. C
10. B

11. C
12. B
13. A
14. D
15. A

16. B
17. A
18. A
19. A
20. A

21. B
22. B
23. D
24. C
25. D

ECONOMICS
EXAMINATION SECTION

TEST 1

DIRECTIONS: Each question or incomplete statement is followed by several suggested answers or completions. Select the one that *BEST* answers the question or completes the statement. *PRINT THE LETTER OF THE CORRECT ANSWER IN THE SPACE AT THE RIGHT.*

1. An outstanding development, related to the marketing of consumer goods, which has taken place since World War II is a(n) 1.___
   A. decline in auto sales
   B. rapid expansion of consumer credit
   C. leveling off of disposable personal income
   D. uninterrupted decline in personal savings

2. A comparison of the gross national product, the national income, and the personal income of a nation for any given year would reveal that 2.___
   A. the gross national product expresses the monetary value of the nation's capital goods
   B. personal income is usually the smallest of the three figures
   C. national income includes allowances for depreciation or capital consumption expenditures
   D. personal income excludes both personal and corporate savings of a nation

3. As a result of the shifting occupational structure of the United States, the greatest decrease in the labor force percentage-wise occurred in 3.___
   A. the extractive industries
   B. the manufacturing industries
   C. trade and transportation
   D. government service

4. Which one of the following statements concerning the economic effect of the Second World War on the United States is most accurate? 4.___
   A. The War changed us from a creditor to a debtor nation.
   B. We became a net exporter of raw materials instead of a net importer.
   C. We became a net importer of raw materials instead of a net exporter.
   D. The War made us dependent upon African commodities and markets in place of those of Latin America.

5. Which one of the following items is a probable cause of the other three? 5.___
   A. Development of nuclear fission
   B. Decline of the coal industry
   C. Discovery of uranium and plutonium deposits
   D. Decentralization of industry

6. Under the national emergency provisions of the Labor Management Relations Act of 1947 (Taft-Hartley), 6.___
   A. mediation of the dispute may be ordered by the President of the United States
   B. seizure of affected plants by the federal government is authorized if Congress concurs
   C. the federal government may obtain an injunction delaying a strike for eighty days
   D. compulsory arbitration may be invoked by the President

7. Which one of the following pairs is matched *INCORRECTLY?* 7.___
   A. Constant dollars - Price indexes
   B. Auto licenses - "Ability to pay" principle of taxation
   C. Net national product - Gross national product minus depreciation
   D. Secular stagnation - Keynes-Hansen thesis

8. The basic purpose of our federal and state conservation programs has been to 8.___
   A. preserve our natural resources for the purpose of ultimately deriving an important source of income for the federal budget
   B. aid the consumer by increasing the production of consumer goods and thus reducing prices
   C. help make our internal waterways, our forests, and our watersheds self-supporting and, thus, reduce the burden on government
   D. protect the public interest against treatment of our natural resources solely as sources of immediate income and not as capital assets

9. If the names Joseph A. Schumpeter, Wesley C. Mitchell, and A. F. Burns were mentioned in a discussion, the subject matter under discussion would be <u>most</u> likely that of 9.___
   A. money and banking
   B. business cycles
   C. housing
   D. social security

10. One of the major economic characteristics of the United States in the 1920's was a(n) 10.___
    A. low national income
    B. high degree of unemployment
    C. growing concentration of the control of industry
    D. increasing proportionate distribution of our national wealth among farmers, workers, and businessmen

11. Which one of the following aspects of the government's farm program has resulted in government ownership of large stocks of agricultural products? 11.___
   A. Nonrecourse loans
   B. "Soil bank" payments
   C. Export subsidies
   D. National School Lunch program

12. An economist known for supporting the idea that some inflation is not necessarily an economic evil, is 12.___
   A. Marcus Nadler
   B. G. Rowland Collins
   C. Paul A. Samuelson
   D. Sumner H. Slichter

13. Which one of the following is *TRUE* with regard to the consumer cooperative movement? 13.___
   A. The number of shares which one may buy is usually unlimited.
   B. Only members may purchase goods from the cooperative.
   C. All members of a consumers' cooperative have equal voting rights.
   D. An annual dividend based on profits is paid on each share.

14. Which one of the following was *MOST* unlike the other three in his social and political outlook? 14.___
   A. Robert Owen
   B. Mikhail Bakunin
   C. Louis Blanc
   D. Charles Fourier

15. The concept of the "economic man" in the history of economic thought relates to an individual who seeks to 15.___
   A. further his economic self-interest above anything else
   B. create a balance and equilibrium among the factors of consumption, production, distribution,and exchange
   C. make the superiority of capitalism over socialism a reality
   D. interpret politics mainly in the light of economic factors

16. According to the law of monopoly price, a monopolist will charge that price which will give him the 16.___
   A. greatest net profit
   B. highest price that consumers are willing to pay
   C. lowest cost of production
   D. greatest number of sales of his product

17. During the first decade of the 20th century, the American farmer enjoyed a period of comparatively sustained prosperity despite the fact that 17.___
   A. the number of his domestic competitors was increasing

B. he was rapidly losing a large part of his foreign market
C. his political influence was waning
D. there was a deflationary movement after the discovery of gold in the Yukon

18. Unemployment which occurs when workers move from job to job is known as 18.___
A. frictional unemployment
B. seasonal unemployment
C. technological unemployment
D. cyclical unemployment

19. Which one of the following is *INCORRECTLY* matched? 19.___
A. Joan Robinson - Imperfect Competition
B. Edward H. Chamberlain - Monopolistic Competition
C. Thorstein Veblen - Institutional Economics
D. Francis A. Walker - Welfare Economics

20. According to the theories of J.M. Keynes, which one of the following factors is *LEAST* important in determining the level of employment and national income? 20.___
A. Liquidity preference.
B. Wage bargaining between employers and employees
C. The propensity to consume
D. The marginal efficiency of capital

21. Which one of the following is *NOT* true concerning the various forms of business enterprise? 21.___
A. Although approximately one-half of all manufacturing businesses in the United States are operated by single entrepeneurs, they account for only approximately ten percent of the manufactured output.
B. Convertible bonds are those bonds which may be converted into income bonds on which interest is payable only if there are earnings by the corporation.
C. Some securities are exempt from "blue-sky" laws because they are listed upon recognized stock exchanges.
D. Some states have acted to help partnerships by laws permitting some limitation on the liability of the members.

22. Buying and selling the same commodity at the same time, but in two different markets, to take advantage of differences in the price of the commodity in the two places at the same instant, is known as 22.___
A. hedging
B. a joint operational cost
C. arbitrage
D. an open market operation

23. Which one of the following is *NOT* true concerning the control of credit by the Federal Government? 23.___
A. The Securities and Exchange Commission can raise or

lower margin requirements on stock sales.
B. The Federal Reserve Board places certain restrictions on bank loans on real estate.
C. The Federal Reserve Board may raise or lower the rediscount rate.
D. The Federal Reserve Board does not control consumer credit at present.

24. In the course of production of goods by the modern corporation, marginal costs are those costs which 24.___
A. are considered variable costs
B. are considered fixed costs
C. result from a one-unit addition to output
D. are obtained by dividing the total cost of production by the number of units produced

25. The optimum economic situation in regard to population in any country is 25.___
A. that number of people whose labor will produce the largest possible per capita product
B. the greatest number of people that country has ever had
C. that time in a country's history of population where there has been developed the highest per capita income
D. one in which there is a balance between industrial and agricultural workers

KEY (CORRECT ANSWERS)

1. B
2. B
3. B
4. C
5. A

6. C
7. B
8. D
9. B
10. C

11. A
12. D
13. C
14. B
15. A

16. A
17. B
18. A
19. D
20. B

21. B
22. C
23. A
24. C
25. A

TEST 2

DIRECTIONS: Each question or incomplete statement is followed by several suggested answers or completions. Select the one that *BEST* answers the question or completes the statement. *PRINT THE LETTER OF THE CORRECT ANSWER IN THE SPACE AT THE RIGHT.*

1. With which one of the following is the "iron law of wages" *MOST* closely associated? 1.___
   A. David Ricardo B. Leon Walras
   C. Adam Smith D. Alfred Marshall

2. A school of economic thought which had as its central doctrine the idea of the "net surplus" or the "product net" was the 2.___
   A. physiocrat B. classical
   C. institutional D. mathematical

3. Which one of the following is a *CORRECT* statement in regard to the Federal Deposit Insurance Corporation? 3.___
   A. Insurance of bank deposits was included in the original Federal Reserve Act.
   B. The insurance maximum is currently $ 100,000 on each insured.
   C. The F.D.I.C. obtains its funds from government appropriations.
   D. All banks which have savings accounts are automatically eligible for F.D.I.C. protection.

4. Which one of the following statements concerning elasticity of demand in a system of private enterprise is *TRUE?* 4.___
   A. The demand for the product of each firm is elastic in a perfectly competitive industry.
   B. Demand becomes inelastic in a completely monopolistic situation.
   C. Elasticity of demand is increased when some firms in an industry obtain strong consumer preference.
   D. Elasticity of demand is increased in an imperfectly competitive industry.

5. Which one of the following is *NOT* a provision of the Taft-Hartley Law? 5.___
   A. Unions engaging in strikes or other activities which violate contracts with employers are subject to damage suits in the federal courts.
   B. Both prosecuting and judicial functions in administering the Taft-Hartley Law are combined in the NLRB.

C. At least sixty days' notice must be given by unions and employers before existing contracts may be modified or terminated.
D. Featherbedding is included among labor practices prohibited by the law.

6. In a consumer problems unit, which one of the following would be a valid concept to develop? 6.___
A. In a full employment economy, the problem of poverty virtually disappears.
B. In general, low national income is caused by low economic productivity.
C. In the United States, the percentage of families with very low incomes (below $10,000) is just about the same as the percentage of families at the other end of the scale with high incomes (above $100,000).
D. In modern industrial countries, the distribution of income before taxes is slowly becoming more unequal.

7. Which one of the following is most like the original Rochdale cooperative? 7.___
A. A consumer-owned cooperative
B. A retailers' cooperative
C. A farmers' marketing cooperative
D. A dairymen's cooperative creamery

8. A teacher puts these figures on the board: 8.___

Plant Capacity	Unit Cost
500	$ 6.50
3,000	4.90
30,000	5.10

He is probably trying to demonstrate the
A. advantages of large-scale production
B. effect of increased advertising costs upon total costs
C. limitations on the efficiency of large-scale production
D. effect of higher labor costs upon costs of production

9. Which item is a prerequisite for the functioning of the other three? 9.___
A. Assembly line production B. Sub-contracting
C. Standardization of parts D. Automation

10. Workers of the XYZ Baking Company are picketing a chain food store to influence the public to refrain from purchasing the products of the XYZ Baking Company. This is an example of a 10.___
A. primary boycott B. secondary boycott
C. sympathetic strike D. stranger picketing

11. Which one of the following would be termed an illegal demand of unions in collective bargaining proceedings in the United States today? 11.___
    A. Checkoff
    B. Exclusive bargaining shop
    C. Preferential shop
    D. Closed shop

12. Which one of the following is *NOT* a power of the Board of Governors of the Federal Reserve? 12.___
    A. It may vary within limits the reserve requirements of member banks.
    B. It controls the Board of Directors of the 12 Reserve Banks by appointing a majority of each Board.
    C. It has control over the open market policy of the Reserve Banks.
    D. It may review the rediscount rate charged by the Reserve Banks.

13. Which one of the following is the basis for the maintenance of resale prices for trademarked goods? 13.___
    A. Robinson-Patman Act
    B. Sherman Anti-Trust Act
    C. Miller-Tydings Act
    D. Clayton Anti-Trust Act

14. Farm legislation now effective 14.___
    A. mandates price support of basic commodities at a fixed 90% of parity
    B. permits price support on a flexible basis
    C. includes the basic features of the Brannan Plan
    D. dispenses with a referendum in connection with marketing quotas

15. In the decision rendered by the Supreme Court against the Dupont Corporation in 1957, the Clayton Anti-Trust Act was used to attack 15.___
    A. a horizontal combination
    B. a vertical combination
    C. the principle of monopoly price
    D. a natural monopoly

16. Which one of the following series could appropriately be captioned "Consumer Price Index for the First Three Months of 19—?" 16.___

A.	122.2	122.5	123.3
B.	$98.05	$98.53	$98.70
C.	$5,232	$5,236	$5,271
D.	1.2	1.3	2.1

17. Which one of the following is *NOT* correctly associated with the economic philosophy of Adam Smith? 17.___
    A. Belief in the motivating force of enlightened self-interest
    B. Advocacy of a policy of national self-sufficiency
    C. Distinction among rent, wages, and profits

D. Concept of the stationary state

18. John Maynard Keynes' theory of the causes of economic depressions centered about 18.___
A. fluctuations in the value of money
B. the relation of savings to investment
C. influence of the growth of monopolies on market price
D. principles derived from statistical analysis of business cycles

19. Which one of the following concepts is emphasized in the writings of Veblen? 19.___
A. Importance of economic institutions
B. Motivating force of self-interest
C. Immutability of economic institutions
D. Need to restrict the right of private property

20. Which one of the following was included among the ideas of Thomas Robert Malthus? 20.___
A. Opposition to the then current English Poor Laws
B. Support of Godwin's theory of human perfectibility
C. Recognition of then current population trends in the United States as exceptions to his theory
D. Support of the pessimistic approach to economics expressed in the writings of Adam Smith

21. Of the following groups of names, which combination is *BEST* associated with the reduction of tariff rates in the United States? 21.___
A. Walker and Underwood
B. Fordney and Walker
C. McKinley and Underwood
D. Aldrich and Dingley

22. The controversy over "right-to-work" laws is related to the general problem of revision of the Taft-Hartley Act in that under that act 22.___
A. union security provisions in labor-management contracts may be prohibited completely by state action
B. union security provisions in labor-management contracts may be prohibited by state action in relation to intrastate business only
C. workers can not be discharged for failure to pay union dues
D. "right-to-work" protection for workers is omitted from the list of subjects on which collective bargaining is compulsory

23. The Labor-Management Realtions (Taft-Hartley) Act of 1947 23.___
A. forbids the use of injunctions in labor disputes
B. established the National Labor Relations Board
C. prohibits union shops
D. prohibits jurisdictional strikes

24. Which one of the following areas was not affected by the operation of the Point Four Program? 24.___
    A. Africa B. Latin America C. Europe D. The Near East

25. Which one of the following may be a factor in bringing on further inflation in the economy of the United States? 25.___
    A. The deficit of the government of the United States
    B. The rise in productivity resulting from automation
    C. Inventory liquidation by large corporations
    D. Statistical projection of current consumer price index trends

KEY (CORRECT ANSWERS)

1. A
2. A
3. B
4. A
5. B

6. B
7. A
8. C
9. C
10. B

11. D
12. B
13. C
14. B
15. B

16. A
17. B
18. B
19. A
20. A

21. A
22. A
23. D
24. C
25. A

TEST 3

DIRECTIONS: Each question or incomplete statement is followed by several suggested answers or completions. Select the one that *BEST* answers the question or completes the statement. *PRINT THE LETTER OF THE CORRECT ANSWER IN THE SPACE AT THE RIGHT.*

1. In a discussion of international trade in wheat, which one of the following would fall in a classification different from the other three? 1.___
   A. India B. Argentine C. Canada D. Australia

2. The controversial Brannan Plan for agriculture proposed 2.___
   A. abandonment of the existing price support program
   B. allowing prices of perishable crops to be set by free action of supply and demand
   C. abandonment of the parity price formula for "basic" commodities
   D. restriction of price support payments to products of which no surplus exists

3. Of the following statements, the one which is a valid generalization concerning the activities of the Federal Trade Commission in preventing unfair methods of competition is: 3.___
   A. The punitive powers of the Commission are limited to the imposition of fines.
   B. Action by the Commission must be based upon proof of damage to competitors or public.
   C. The Commission is an investigating body; to effect action its findings must be incorporated in court orders.
   D. The Commission acts only in regard to unfair methods of competition carried on in interstate commerce.

4. Which of the following functions is *NOT* within the jurisdiction of the Securities and Exchange Commission? 4.___
   A. It has the right to establish the rules for the conduct of business on the security exchanges.
   B. It requires periodic reports (which are open to the public) from corporations whose securities are listed.
   C. It has the power to fix margin requirements.
   D. It may suspend trading on any issue of securities which does not comply with its rules concerning registration.

5\. The ability of a commercial bank to increase its loans and investments depends on its 5.___
   A. required legal reserve B. cash position
   C. excess primary reserves D. outstanding loans and investments

6\. Which one of the causes of economic inequality listed below is *INCORRECTLY* matched with a suggested remedy? 6.___
   A. Inheritances - proportional taxation
   B. War profiteering - price ceilings
   C. Differences in the marginal productivity of labor-minimum wage laws
   D. Unearned increment - the single tax

7\. Which one of the following is now generally considered by economists as least likely to affect consumers' propensity to consume? 7.___
   A. Changes in interest rate for consumer credit
   B. Consumer expectations concerning prices and availability of goods
   C. Changes in pattern of income distribution
   D. Changes in consumers' stocks of liquid assets

8\. The economic term "multiplier" is used to explain the effect of 8.___
   A. investment spending upon national income
   B. consumer saving upon investment spending
   C. consumer saving upon national income
   D. the interest rate upon investment spending

9\. Which one of the following terms is *NOT* associated in economic literature with the theory of imperfect competition? 9.___
   A. Oligopoly
   B. Price leadership
   C. Product differentiation
   D. Representative firm

10\. Which one of the following theories of the business cycle was accepted by Karl Marx? 10.___
   A. The over-investment theory
   B. The under-investment theory
   C. The theory based on variations in the amount of money in circulation
   D. The theory based on overproduction

11\. The "Communist Manifesto" 11.___
   A. was critical of the Utopian Socialists of the nineteenth century
   B. attempted to justify the Communist Revolution which had taken place in Russia in 1917
   C. was a document issued by the Paris Commune
   D. was written by Marx and Fourier

12. Which of the following dates of business crises is *INCORRECTLY* paired with an important causal factor? 12.___
    A. 1837 - land speculation
    B. 1873 - currency inflation
    C. 1921 - loss of European markets
    D. 1929 - stock market speculation

13. The form of business organization known as a limited partnership 13.___
    A. is unused in the United States
    B. permits partners to define the extent of their liability
    C. places restrictions upon the amount of capital that may be invested in a partnership
    D. restricts the number of individuals who may enter into a partnership

14. The history of corporate growth since 1900 has been marked by a 14.___
    A. steady concentration in big companies
    B. uneven periods of concentration and decentralization
    C. little basic change
    D. growth of competition

15. Which of the following *MOST* accurately reflects the present position of American businessmen on tariff protection? 15.___
    A. They are united in opposing decreased tariff barriers.
    B. Executives of some industries with important export markets are giving increasing support to tariff reduction.
    C. Importers favor tariff reduction but other businessmen oppose it.
    D. The N.A.M. reflects majority business opinion in its continued opposition to the trade agreements program.

16. Under presently existing federal legislation, strikes that imperil national health or safety 16.___
    A. are outlawed
    B. are subject to compulsory arbitration
    C. are automatically postponed upon the appointment by the President of a board of inquiry
    D. can be postponed for a limited period by government action

17. Which one of the following is determined by the Consumer Price Index of the Bureau of Labor Statistics? 17.___
    A. Escalator clause B. Wage-differentials

C. Guaranteed annual wage D. Escape clause

18. An investment tax credit (ITC) is normally defined as 18.___
   A. a dollar for dollar credit against any tax liability
   B. a dollar for dollar deduction from other income subject to tax
   C. a percentage credit against any tax liability
   D. only available to 'S' corporations and certain limited partnerships

19. Under the Labor Management Relations Act of 1947 (Taft-Hartley Act), injunctions in labor disputes can be obtained by 19.___
   A. government agencies and employers only
   B. government agencies, employers, or unions
   C. employers and unions only
   D. government agencies only

20. Of the following, which book does *NOT* deal with the problem of conservation? 20.___
   A. ROAD TO SURVIVAL - William Vogt
   B. TVA - DEMOCRACY ON THE MARCH - David Lilienthal
   C. OUR PLUNDERED PLANET - Henry Osborn
   D. GIANTS IN THE EARTH - Ole Rolvaag

21. Which one of the following does *NOT* require intervention by a neutral third party in a labor-management dispute? 21.___
   A. Mediation B. Arbitration
   C. Negotiation D. Compulsory investigation

22. Which of the following did *NOT* characterize the Federal Reserve System when it was founded? It 22.___
   A. prohibited member banks from establishing branches
   B. failed to provide for medium-term credit
   C. promoted the growth of security affiliates
   D. permitted state banks and trust companies to become members

23. A substantial increase in bank holdings of government securities, such as occurred as a result of financing methods in World War II, 23.___
   A. makes it easier for the Federal Reserve System to control credit extended by member banks
   B. limits the ability of the Federal Reserve System to use the open market operation most effectively
   C. has substantially no effect on credit conditions
   D. endangers the solvency of the whole banking system

24. The International Monetary Fund, in order to achieve international monetary cooperation, relies on which of the following techniques? 24.___
1. Bills of exchange
2. Bilateral clearing agreements
3. Direct foreign exchange controls
4. Long-run alterations in the trade balance between one country and another

The *CORRECT* answer is:
A. 1 B. 1,2 C. 2,4 D. 3,4

25. Contemporary economists, in emphasizing the exceptions and qualifications in the operation of the international price mechanism, have <u>not</u> stated that 25.___
A. the balance-of-payments mechanism under the gold standard was less effective than the classical economists had believed
B. a balancing of foreign receipts and expenditures cannot be taken for granted
C. the free market system is not necessarily in the interest of each individual country
D. economic stability requires constant supervision and planning

---

KEY (CORRECT ANSWERS)

1. A
2. B
3. D
4. C
5. C

6. A
7. A
8. A
9. D
10. D

11. A
12. B
13. B
14. A
15. B

16. D
17. A
18. A
19. D
20. D

21. C
22. C
23. B
24. A
25. D

TEST 4

DIRECTIONS: Each question or incomplete statement is followed by several suggested answers or completions. Select the one that *BEST* answers the question or completes the statement. *PRINT THE LETTER OF THE CORRECT ANSWER IN THE SPACE AT THE RIGHT.*

1. Henry George, in PROGRESS AND POVERTY, advocated a single-tax on 1.___
   A. unearned increments B. incomes
   C. inheritance D. land

2. The American economist whose ideas most closely resembled those of J.M. Keynes is 2.___
   A. J.A. Schumpeter B. Frank Knight
   C. George Terborgh D. Alvin Hansen

3. Which one of the following does *NOT* belong in a list of "nationalist" economists? 3.___
   A. Johann H. Von Thunen B. Friedrich List
   C. Henry C. Carey D. Adam Muller

4. The subsistence theory of wages is a corollary of 4.___
   A. Gresham's Law
   B. the Ricardian theory of rent
   C. Smith's theory on the forces of demand and supply
   D. the Malthusian theory of population

5. In his book, THEORY OF BUSINESS ENTERPRISE, which one of the following was *NOT* maintained by Thorstein Veblen? 5.___
   A. Modern society is dominated by the machine
   B. Businessmen frequently work against the interest of production
   C. The machine will cause a division in society - the technicians vs. the businessmen
   D. By 2030 A.D. the machine, through increased productivity, will abolish poverty

6. Which one of the following pairs is *NOT* correctly matched? 6.___
   A. Countervailing power - Alfred Marshall
   B. Self-generating business cycles - Wesley Mitchell
   C. Imperfect competition - Joseph Schumpeter
   D. Investment multiplier - John Keynes

7. The theory that standards of consumption are generally subject to a selection process so rigorous that unfit ones tend to die while the socially desirable ones endure, would be challenged by 7.___

1. John Ruskin
2. Thorstein Veblen
3. J. A. Hobson
4. Stuart Chase

The *CORRECT* combination is:
A. 1,2,4 B. 2,4 C. 2,3,4 D. 3,4

8. A study of economic thought as an integral factor in the development of American culture is 8.___
   A. Dorfman's THE ECONOMIC MIND
   B. Keynes' GENERAL THEORY
   C. Mitchell's BUSINESS CYCLES
   D. Rist's HISTORY OF ECONOMIC DOCTRINES

9. Which one of the following men was *NOT* a contemporary of the other three? 9.___
   A. Karl Marx
   B. Francois Babeuf
   C. Ferdinand Lassalle
   D. Wilhelm Liebknecht

10. The economist <u>most</u> often credited with providing the theoretical base of the institutional school of economics was 10.___
    A. Wesley C. Mitchell
    B. Thorstein Veblen
    C. Karl Marx
    D. Alfred Marshall

11. In a corporation, the group that participates *MOST* directly in forming its policies is the 11.___
    A. stockholders
    B. board of directors
    C. officers of the corporation
    D. bondholders

12. Which of the following statements regarding cooperatives in the United States are *TRUE?* 12.___
    1. Profits are shared according to the amount bought or sold.
    2. Voting power is proportionate to the number of shares owned.
    3. Marketing cooperatives are more popular than consumers cooperatives.
    4. Some states have not yet legalized cooperatives.

    The *CORRECT* combination is:
    A. 1,3 B. 1,4 C. 2,3 D. 2,4

13. When a country depreciates its currency, its exports are 13.___
    A. increased
    B. decreased
    C. stabilized
    D. unaffected

14. The type of business combination that brings together, in one large corporation, companies that manufacture products that are not competitive, but are sold to the same general class of consumers, is an example of 14.___
    A. linear combination
    B. horizontal combination

C. circular combination D. vertical combination

15. Which one of the following is illegal under the Taft-Hartley Act? 15.___
   A. Strikes in essential industries
   B. Featherbedding
   C. The union shop
   D. Unionization of foremen

16. Which statements concerning the powers of the Interstate Commerce Commission are *TRUE?* 16.___
   1. Its jurisdiction extends to buses and trucks engaged in interstate commerce.
   2. It settles disputes involving railroad workers.
   3. It may set both minimum and maximum rates for railroads.
   4. It may set only maximum rates for railroads.

   The *CORRECT* statements are:
   A. 1,2,3 B. 2,4 C. 3,4 D. 1,3

17. Which one of the following is *NOT* included in the determination of the gross national product? 17.___
   A. Total expenditures by the ultimate consumer
   B. Total expenditures of employers for wages
   C. Total expenditures of businessmen for expansion of investment at home and abroad
   D. Total of government expenditures for all purposes

18. Which of the following is the precursor or cause of the other? 18.___
   A. Emphasis on sure money crops
   B. Stratification of class lines
   C. Introduction of tenant farming
   D. Lack of diversification of crops

19. In discussing the topic of standard of living, the important point of emphasis might well be the concept that, in the United States, to give everybody as comfortable a standard of living as that now enjoyed by the most fortunate few, the basic need is for 19.___
   A. more equitable distribution of our present national income
   B. increased levels of production
   C. drastic modification of our income tax structure
   D. reversal of our present population trends

20. Under existing legislation, the federal government 20.___
   A. recognizes an obligation to maintain full employment in the United States
   B. plays no part in the unemployment systems of the states
   C. enforces a federal fair employment practices law

D. disburses uniform unemployment benefits to all workers in interstate commerce

21. The Physiocrats did *NOT* favor 21.___
   A. emphasis on the productive value of agricultural labor that brought new commodities into existence
   B. most of the imports upon which the Mercantilists had relied for regulation of the economic system
   C. the cessation of all public regulation of economic activities
   D. that a regime of individualism, competition,and free trade should be instituted

22. Studies of the corporation by J.K. Gailbraith, David Lilienthal, Adolph E. Berle, Jr.,are alike in that they accept the thesis that 22.___
   A. concentration of economic wealth is on the decline in America
   B. adequate safeguards have been developed for curbing corporate power
   C. the giant corporation is an important force for improving the lot of mankind
   D. competition is more vigorous than it once was

23. In case of bankruptcy, the liability of a partner to creditors 23.___
   A. is to the extent of his paid-in investment in the partnership
   B. is for the full amount of money he has agreed to invest in the partnership
   C. does not extend beyond the resources of the partnership
   D. is personal liability for the debts of the partership

24. In the event of bankruptcy of a corporation, how are assets distributed? 24.___
   A. Preferred stockholders are paid in full and then the bondholders
   B. Common stockholders are paid in full and then the bondholders
   C. Common stockholders are paid in full and then the preferred stockholders
   D. Bondholders are paid in full and then the stockholders

25. Which one of the following American economic writers is *INCORRECTLY* paired with the title of the book? 25.___
   A. Ida Tarbell - WEALTH AGAINST COMMONWEALTH
   B. Edward Bellamy - LOOKING BACKWARD
   C. Henry George - PROGRESS AND POVERTY
   D. Thorstein Veblen - THEORY OF THE LEISURE CLASS

KEY (CORRECT ANSWERS)

1. D
2. D
3. A
4. D
5. D

6. A
7. A
8. A
9. B
10. B

11. B
12. A
13. A
14. C
15. B

16. D
17. B
18. C
19. B
20. A

21. B
22. C
23. D
24. D
25. A

TEST 5

DIRECTIONS: Each question or incomplete statement is followed by several suggested answers or completions. Select the one that *BEST* answers the question or completes the statement. *PRINT THE LETTER OF THE CORRECT ANSWER IN THE SPACE AT THE RIGHT.*

1. When Federal Reserve banks buy securities in the open market, 1.___
   A. business loans are discouraged
   B. the reserves of commercial banks are decreased
   C. the rediscount rate is increased
   D. the lending power of commercial banks is increased

2. Under the 1936 Clayton Act amendment, called the Robinson-Patman Act, 2.___
   A. price concessions to large firms by manufacturers are outlawed
   B. re-sale price maintenance by retailers is authorized by law
   C. the Federal Trade Commission may directly regulate false advertising
   D. price discounts to large buyers are permitted if proportionate to cost differentials

3. Which one of the following statements does *NOT* correctly describe the functions of the S.E.Ç.? 3.___
   A. It attempts to maintain a fair market price for stocks and bonds.
   B. It requires registration of stock exchanges with the Commission.
   C. It aims to prevent price manipulations by market operators.
   D. It provides controls over the extension of credit for security speculation.

4. Which of the following was the most valid and pertinent economic argument in favor of granting foreign aid under the so-called Point Four program? 4.___
   A. International trade is largest between developed industrial nations.
   B. Large capital loans and grants are the only way to effect substantial permanent improvement in the standard of living of under-developed countries.
   C. International trade is largest between developed and under-developed countries.
   D. Increasing industry in under-developed countries will decrease our trade with them but this is a

necessary price in the struggle against communism.

5. In statistical presentations related to national income, which one of the following figures is *ALWAYS* the largest for any given year? 5.___
   A. Personal income
   B. Net national product
   C. National income
   D. Gross national product

6. With which of the following terms are the contributions of John M. Keynes to economic theory <u>most</u> closely associated? 6.___
   A. Law of comparative advantage
   B. Marginal utility
   C. Employment equilibrium
   D. Monopolistic competition

7. The theory of wages which maintains that under competitive conditions wages are determined by demand and supply, at a point equal to the marginal productivity of labor, was set forth by 7.___
   A. David Ricardo
   B. John Stuart Mill
   C. Alfred Marshall
   D. John Bates Clark

8. Which group contains the names of economists in the same school of economic thought? 8.___
   A. Adam Smith - Friedrich List
   B. Thomas Mun - Anne Robert Turgot
   C. Thorstein Veblen - Wesley Mitchell
   D. Leon Walras - Karl Marx

9. Which one of the following should, theoretically, have a different effect upon the economy from the other three? 9.___
   A. Increase of margin requirements for stock market purchasing
   B. Purchase of government securities by a Federal Reserve bank
   C. Raising of Federal Reserve rediscount rate
   D. Increase in reserve requirements for member banks in a Federal Reserve district

10. Under conditions of full employment, raising taxes to a point where a budgetary surplus is created will 10.___
    A. reduce any existing tendency toward inflation
    B. increase any existing tendency toward inflation
    C. stabilize the economy at a high price level
    D. have a negligible effect

11. Which of the following statements belong to a pattern of economic development which was formed in the South during 1865 - 1900? 11.___
    1. Cotton was perpetuated as the main crop through a crop-lien system of financing.

2. Share-cropping provided a system of labor that enabled large numbers of plantations to continue.
3. The great planters were successful in re-establishing agriculture on its former large-scale basis.
4. Small yeoman farmers with little funds bought up the choicest plots of bankrupted plantations.

The *CORRECT* combination is:
A. 2,3,4 B. 1,2,3 C. 1,2,4 D. 1,3,4

12. Which one of the following statements about farm income and prices since 1865 is *FALSE?* 12.___
A. Since 1947, the number of farming units has increased steadily.
B. After the Civil War the farmer sold at low prices in the world market and bought at high prices in the protected home market.
C. Acreage control and soil conservation have been used as a means of keeping farm prices steady by limiting production.
D. Parity payments have attempted to adjust farmers' income to workers' income.

13. Which of the following are *CORRECT* statements regarding the American farm problem? 13.___
1. In 1860, agriculture represented about half the national wealth.
2. In 1880, a majority of American farmers owned their own land.
3. The farmer received a decreasing share of the national income between 1860 and 1930.
4. Between 1890 and 1930, an increasing number of farms was mortgaged.

The *CORRECT* combination is:
A. 1,2 B. 1,3,4 C. 2,3,4 D. 1,2,3,4

14. The Brannan Plan differed from the farm policies under the New Deal in that under it 14.___
A. prices of perishable farm products would have been allowed to rise or fall according to the law of supply and demand
B. parity prices would have been more flexible
C. farmers would have had no voice in determining acreage allotments
D. payments to the farmers would have to be greater during periods of prosperity than during periods of depression

15. The AFL differed from the Knights of Labor in that the AFL believed that 15.___
A. the national structure should be built on strong local unions united into city and state federations
B. unions should base their programs on utopian objectives

C. unions should not dissipate their energies in fighting for the improvement of the position of women in industry
D. the unlimited immigration of European laborers would add to the strength of the American labor movement

16. Which statement concerning labor *BEST* describes the attitude of most Americans in the years immediately after the Civil War? 16.___
A. They welcomed the entry of labor into politics.
B. There was little hostility to the closed shop.
C. Picketing and the boycott were regarded as legitimate weapons of labor.
D. Public opinion tended to be more hostile to labor than to capital.

17. Organized labor at first opposed minimum wage legislation because they claimed such laws 17.___
A. violated the fourteenth amendment
B. were an undue exercise of the police power of the state
C. interfered with labor's right to enter into contracts freely
D. tended to lower the general wage scale

18. Which one of the following provisions of the Social Security Act is administered by the federal government exclusively? 18.___
A. Old-age assistance
B. Old-age and survivors insurance
C. Unemployment compensation
D. Assistance for dependent children

19. The chief technological advance in recent years in the field of mass production has been the 19.___
A. application of scientific management
B. harnessing of atomic energy to industrial machines
C. development of the "belt-line" using computerized robotics
D. development of automation

20. The relationship of a stock holder to a corporation is that of a(n) ________. 20.___
A. owner
B. debtor
C. creditor
D. manager

21. In teaching the forms of business organization, which of the following terms would the teacher be *LEAST* likely to explain? 21.___
A. Limited liability
B. Absentee ownership
C. Equity capital
D. Reserve ratio

22. The statement that imperfect competition prevails in a given industry means that prices in that industry are determined 22.___
   A. by government regulation
   B. by a single firm with a monopoly position
   C. solely by conditions in the market
   D. by the competing firms' decisions

23. Which of the following was *NOT* an economic consequence of the Fordney-McCumber Tariff Act of 1921? 23.___
   A. It encouraged the growth of monopolies in the United States.
   B. The tariff commission gave flexibility to the schedules,thereby equalizing production costs at home and abroad.
   C. It prevented Europe from paying her war debt to us in the form of goods.
   D. Foreign countries introduced retaliatory tariffs.

24. The tax in the United States which *MOST* closely meets the needs of a sound tax system is the 24.___
   A. personal income tax B. excess profits tax
   C. death and inheritance tax D. excise tax

25. In teaching the topic of exchange, a point of emphasis would be the fact that at least nine-tenths of all transactions (in terms of value) are accomplished by the use of 25.___
   A. Federal Reserve notes B. promissory notes
   C. checks D. bills of exchange

KEY (CORRECT ANSWERS)

1. C
2. D
3. A
4. A
5. D

6. C
7. C
8. C
9. B
10. A

11. C
12. A
13. D
14. A
15. A

16. D
17. D
18. B
19. D
20. A

21. D
22. D
23. B
24. A
25. C

ECONOMICS

EXAMINATION SECTION

TEST 1

DIRECTIONS: Each question or incomplete statement is followed by several suggested answers or completions. Select the one that BEST answers the question or completes the statement. *PRINT THE LETTER OF THE CORRECT ANSWER IN THE SPACE AT THE RIGHT.*

1. The concept of equilibrium involves the idea that 1.___
   A. the economy can operate with no fluctuations
   B. fluctuations tend to be self-correcting
   C. there must be perfect competition for it to work
   D. the economy can operate with fluctuation
   E. the economy can operate even in a state of monopoly

2. Limitations upon freedom of occupational choice in the United States include 2.___
   A. inequality of income distribution
   B. discrimination in employment
   C. inequality of educational or training opportunities
   D. inadequate vocational guidance and apprentice training
   E. all of the above

3. Inequality of income is needed in an economy to 3.___
   I. create an aristocracy of wealth
   II. make savings available for investment
   III. persuade people to work harder
   IV. provide a strong national defense
   V. make a nation self-sufficient

   The CORRECT answer is:
   A. I, II B. I, III C. I, III, V
   D. III, IV, V E. II, III

4. Modern industrial society is based PRIMARILY upon which of the following? 4.___
   I. Forests II. Coal III. Gold
   IV. Iron ore V. Petroleum

   The CORRECT answer is:
   A. I, II, III B. II, IV, V C. I, III, IV
   D. I, III, V E. II, III, IV

5. Place these stages of economic development in sequence from the EARLIEST to the LATEST: 5.___
   I. Machine technology and industrial capitalism
   II. Hunting and food-gathering
   III. Plow-agriculture and irrigation
   IV. Pastoralism and digging-stick agriculture
   V. Commercial capitalism

   The CORRECT answer is:
   A. II, III, IV, I, V B. II, III, IV, V, I
   C. II, IV, III, V, I D. IV, II, III, I, V
   E. IV, II, III, V, I

6. The price system tells businessmen how much of what to produce if 6.___
   A. workable competition exists in the market
   B. consumers buy on the basis of advertising only
   C. income is equally distributed only
   D. income is unequally distributed
   E. workable competition does not exist in the market

7. Arrange the following great economic thinkers chronologically: 7.___
   I. John Maynard Keynes
   II. Adam Smith
   III. Karl Marx
   IV. David Ricardo
   V. Thorstein Veblen

   The CORRECT answer is:
   A. II, III, IV, I, V
   B. II, IV, III, V, I
   C. II, III, IV, V, I
   D. IV, II, III, I, V
   E. IV, II, III, V, I

8. Our economic system transforms competition into cooperation by 8.___
   A. freedom of contract
   B. intervention of the government
   C. operation of the price system in commodity markets
   D. all of the above
   E. none of the above

9. By *induced investment* is meant 9.___
   A. changes in investment which result from a change in the Net National Product (NNP)
   B. the fact that increased saving may sometimes result in increased investment
   C. investment made as a result of government orders
   D. an increase in investment which results from technological change
   E. an increase in investment which results from demographical change

10. By the *paradox of thrift* is meant the fact that 10.___
   A. positive saving will always mean unemployment
   B. if changes in investment are induced by changes in Net National Product (NNP), then a decision on the part of people to save more might result in their actually saving less
   C. if the economy is at full employment, a decision on the part of people to save more might produce an inflationary gap
   D. saving stimulates investment spending so as to worsen an inflationary spiral
   E. saving must always equal investment

11. *Liquidity preference* refers to the 11.___
   A. desire of banks to avoid long-term loans
   B. evaluation of cash as against other forms of asset holdings

C. relationship between inventory holdings and the level of consumer demand
D. desire to liquidate ownership of producer durables and inventories in the face of declining consumption
E. rising trend in the consumption of alcoholic beverages

12. Which of the following transfer payments is EXCLUDED from the computation of national income? 12.___
A. Payment for an intermediary good
B. Payment for a service rendered by a soldier to the government
C. Payment of interest on a government bond
D. Payment of interest on a General Motors bond
E. Undistributed corporation profits

13. A tariff for protection against the competition of cheap, foreign labor provides a short-run benefit for 13.___
A. the protected workers
B. all workers
C. all consumers
D. unions
E. the government

14. A factor which did NOT contribute to the postwar *dollar shortage* was the 14.___
A. frequent depreciation of currencies by the dollar-shortage countries
B. wartime destruction of productive facilities in Europe and Asia
C. efforts by Europeans and Asians to live beyond their means
D. faster technological progress in dollar countries than elsewhere
E. rebuilding of war-torn countries

15. Which of the following statements is FALSE? 15.___
A. Tax reduction tends to stimulate income.
B. Tax reduction tends to increase personal consumption.
C. Tax reduction tends to increase personal saving.
D. Whatever else tax reduction does, the increases in personal consumption resulting from tax reductions must stimulate income.
E. If tax reductions cause personal saving to increase, then Net National Product will fail.

16. If the level of spending increases, with the quantity of money held constant, then 16.___
A. the velocity of circulation of money must have increased
B. the amount of real national output must have increased
C. either the velocity of money circulation or the amount of real national output must have increased, or both
D. the amount of real national output must have decreased
E. either the velocity of money circulation must have increased, or the amount of real national output must have decreased, or both

17. If the Federal Reserve authorities wished to pursue an expansionary monetary policy, it would be CORRECT for them to 17.___
   A. raise the discount rate to discourage hoarding by the public
   B. raise reserve requirements to eliminate any excess reserves held by the Member banks
   C. raise margin requirements to discourage wasteful speculation
   D. sell securities on the open market to drive interest rates down
   E. do none of the above

18. An expansionary monetary policy adopted by a central bank will be UNSUCCESSFUL if 18.___
   A. prices do not increase
   B. saving on the part of the public does not decrease
   C. investment spending is not changed by a change in the interest rate
   D. the inflationary tendency which prompted this policy is not checked
   E. no decrease in the price of government bonds occurs

19. The C plus I plus G schedule would tend to be shifted up by 19.___
   A. an increase in taxes
   B. a decrease in government spending
   C. an increase in interest rates
   D. open-market sales by the central bank
   E. none of the above

20. MOST of the very large United States federal debt outstanding arose as the result of 20.___
   A. war
   B. depressions
   C. borrowing to meet interest charges on previous debts
   D. borrowing from abroad
   E. welfare payments

21. In the following table, indicate the number showing the interval in which demand is elastic. 21.___

	P	q
	1	100
I.	3	60
II.	8	30
III.	15	10
IV.	30	5
V.	50	4

The CORRECT answer is:
   A. I   B. II   C. III   D. IV   E. V

22. Using the same table as in the above question, indicate the number showing the interval in which demand is of unitary elasticity. 22.___
The CORRECT interval is:
A. I B. II C. III D. IV E. V

23. When the American Government borrowed in order to finance World War II, it thereby 23.___
A. shifted the economic burden to future generations who would have to pay the interest and principal
B. intensified the danger of national bankruptcy
C. in no sense shifted the burden of the war on future generations
D. placed the American people, though to a lesser degree, in the same difficult position as the British were placed by the war-time borrowing of their government from the United States and other foreign governments
E. lessened the danger of national bankruptcy

24. The existence of a large internally held public debt has 24.___
A. no effect on the nation as a whole
B. creates the danger of national bankruptcy
C. has no effect on the nation as a whole, but does affect certain special interest groups
D. is likely to depress the level of consumption and, hence, lower the equilibrium Net National Product (NNP)
E. is likely to make for greater inequality in the distribution of incomes and to dampen work incentive

25. The risks due to speculative production tend to be increased by 25.___
A. improved transportation
B. improved market information
C. monopoly
D. the roundabout method of production
E. none of the above

KEY (CORRECT ANSWERS)

1. B	6. A	11. B	16. A	21. C
2. E	7. B	12. A	17. E	22. D
3. E	8. D	13. A	18. B	23. C
4. B	9. A	14. A	19. E	24. C
5. C	10. B	15. E	20. A	25. D

TEST 2

DIRECTIONS: Each question or incomplete statement is followed by several suggested answers or completions. Select the one that BEST answers the question or completes the statement. *PRINT THE LETTER OF THE CORRECT ANSWER IN THE SPACE AT THE RIGHT.*

1. To increase output, we MUST do which of the following? Increase 1.___
   I. hours of work
   II. the labor force
   III. output capacity
   IV. leisure time
   V. fringe benefits

   The CORRECT answer is:
   A. I, II, III
   B. I, II, IV
   C. I, III, V
   D. II, III, IV
   E. I, II, III, IV, V

2. The efficiency of production depends upon 2.___
   A. the division of labor and exchange
   B. mass production and mechanization
   C. automation and cybernetics
   D. all of the above
   E. none of the above

3. The accumulation of capital in an economy means the 3.___
   A. amount of money that is saved
   B. growth of output capacity
   C. rise in values on the stock market
   D. amount of money that is invested
   E. rise in values on the realty market

4. The amount of natural resources is 4.___
   I. fixed and unchanging
   II. dependent upon the level of technology
   III. subject to periodic fluctuations
   IV. subject to depletion
   V. proportional to government investment and subsidy

   The CORRECT answer is:
   A. I, II, V
   B. I, III
   C. II, III
   D. II, IV
   E. II, V

5. World population has increased because 5.___
   A. the birth rate has risen sharply
   B. the death rate has fallen sharply
   C. people are not practicing birth control
   D. abortion is illegal in almost all countries
   E. there are more multiple births today due to special drugs

6. The industrial revolution 6.___
   I. had nothing to do with world population increase
   II. did not develop where slavery was the basis of the economy
   III. has not influenced most of the people of the world
   IV. developed first in Britain and spread East and West
   V. has, to all practical purposes, ceased

   The CORRECT answer is:
   A. I, III, V B. I, II C. II, III
   D. II, IV E. II, III, IV, V

7. Living standards depend upon 7.___
   A. the number of people in an area
   B. the ability to produce commodities
   C. the ability to utilize commodities
   D. all of the above
   E. none of the above

8. The law of diminishing returns means that 8.___
   A. the more people work, the less is produced
   B. if one factor of production increases more slowly, eventually there will be a decline in productivity
   C. as population increases geometrically, food production increases arithmetically
   D. as labor increases, production per person declines
   E. as labor decreases, production per person rises

9. The United States Government prefers to sell defense bonds to individuals rather than to banks because the 9.___
   A. average person hoards his high wages in times of prosperity
   B. banks are reluctant to invest large sums of money in such bonds
   C. tendency of such sales is to avert inflation
   D. administration fears the domination of the Government by banking interests
   E. interest rate will be lower

10. In teaching the topic of exchange, a point of emphasis would be the fact that at least nine-tenths of all transactions (in terms of value) are accomplished by the use of 10.___
   A. Federal Reserve notes B. promissory notes
   C. checks D. bills of exchange
   E. certificates of deposit

11. The tax in the United States which MOST closely meets the needs of a sound tax system is the _____ tax. 11.___
   A. personal income B. excess profits
   C. death and inheritance D. excise
   E. sales

12. Money consists of 12.___
    I. legal tender *only*
    II. generally acceptable symbols of claims upon commodities
    III. only gold and silver
    IV. a medium of exchange and measure of value
    V. currency but not checks

    The CORRECT answer is:
    A. I, III B. I, IV C. II, IV
    D. III, V E. I, IV

13. Pre-Keynesian thinking among most economists considered that full employment was the rule because 13.___
    I. according to Say's law, *supply creates its own demand*
    II. prices and wages were becoming less flexible
    III. the interest rate in a free market tends to equalize saving and investment
    IV. barriers to trade were growing after World War I
    V. prices and wages were becoming more flexible

    The CORRECT answer is:
    A. I, IV, V B. I, II C. II, IV
    D. II, III E. I, III, V

14. Free economic goods are those 14.___
    A. which are not important
    B. given to us by our parents
    C. given to us by the government
    D. given to us by nature and requiring no effort to make usable
    E. all of the above

15. The economist needs to know 15.___
    A. only mathematics because economics deals only with quantities
    B. mainly economic theory because economic behavior is common sense
    C. mainly the development of economic thought and institutions
    D. a minimum about human behavior plus economics
    E. as much as possible about the universe including, especially, economics and statistics

16. Economizing is necessary because 16.___
    A. there is not enough money for everybody
    B. resources are scarce in relation to human desires
    C. it is immoral for things to be wasted
    D. standards of value must be established
    E. it is necessary to distribute the wealth more evenly

17. Division of labor is USUALLY defined as 17.___
    A. everyone doing the same amount of work
    B. compartmentalization
    C. specialization
    D. every one doing the same kind of work
    E. mechanization

18. The factors of production are USUALLY considered to be 18.___
I. technology II. land III. labor
IV. climate V. capital

The CORRECT answer is:
A. II, III, IV B. III, IV, V C. I, II, III
D. II, III, V E. I, IV, V

19. Economics is a social science because 19.___
A. tables and graphs are used
B. theory and empirical evidence are related
C. the scientific method is applied to human behavior
D. it deals with the allocation of scarce resources to material ends
E. none of the above

20. In terms of numbers, the form of business unit MOST frequently found in the United States today is the 20.___
A. individual, or single, proprietorship
B. partnership
C. small corporation
D. giant corporation
E. middle corporation

21. The term *limited liability* is frequently used in describing the characteristics of a corporation. 21.___
It means the following:
A. Any officer of the corporation is strictly limited in his ability to speak for the corporation and commit it to any liability
B. Once a shareholder has paid for his stock, he has no further financial obligation, regardless of how much trouble the corporation gets into
C. The corporation's liability to pay dividends to its stockholders is a limited one since it is required to pay them only if it has earned a profit
D. There are certain obligations which a corporation can legally refuse to pay
E. The corporation has only a limited obligation to meet claims made by any single person or firm against it (provided it has acted within the scope of its charter) so that there is some protection for its assets and financial position

22. A corporation's obligation to pay interest on bonds it has issued may be PROPERLY described as follows: 22.___
A. Interest must be paid regardless of whether a profit has been earned or not
B. Interest must be paid whenever a profit has been earned
C. Interest need not be paid even if a profit has been earned, but it must be paid before any dividend is paid

D. Normally, interest ranks ahead of dividends, but there are some circumstances in which a dividend can be paid without payment of bond interest
E. Interest ranks behind dividends and is paid only after dividends have been paid in full

23. The MAIN reason why indirect or *capital-using* methods of production have not displaced direct methods in economically underdeveloped areas of the world is: 23.____
A. The governments of such areas have not issued enough money to finance indirect methods
B. People do not realize that the indirect methods would produce more consumption goods
C. There are no indirect methods that would actually produce more consumption goods
D. Such areas do not have a properly functioning price system
E. The adoption of such indirect methods would involve a sacrifice of present consumption

24. The economic problem of how goods shall be produced is that of 24.____
A. finding out how much product will be obtained when given quantities of factors of production are put to work together in the most effective known manner
B. having a mechanism that will somehow reveal what goods people really want to be produced
C. getting the existing factors of production distributed among different occupations to best produce whatever goods the community wants
D. deciding how the goods that have been produced shall be distributed among the people who made those goods
E. none of the above

25. An economic theory is scientific 25.____
I. even if it requires many assumptions and has no relation to the actual operation of the economy
II. if it is consistent, even if it has little value for forecasting
III. if it is internally consistent and has a minimum of assumptions
IV. if it has considerable usefulness in forecasting
V. it is internally consistent and has a maximum of assumptions

The CORRECT answer is:
A. I, II, V B. I, III C. II, III
D. III, IV E. III, IV, V

KEY (CORRECT ANSWERS)

1. A	6. D	11. A	16. B	21. B
2. D	7. D	12. C	17. C	22. A
3. B	8. B	13. A	18. D	23. E
4. D	9. C	14. D	19. C	24. E
5. B	10. C	15. E	20. A	25. D

TEST 3

DIRECTIONS: Each question or incomplete statement is followed by several suggested answers or completions. Select the one that BEST answers the question or completes the statement. *PRINT THE LETTER OF THE CORRECT ANSWER IN THE SPACE AT THE RIGHT.*

1. The *accelerator* principle of the business cycle means that 1.___
   A. a slight increase in demand will step up a much larger increase in production
   B. an increase in production, followed up by efficient advertising techniques, will accelerate an increase in demand
   C. the severity of a depression will be accelerated if the government does not step in with a public works program
   D. the upward trend of business depends upon a quickened activity in the sale of stocks and bonds

2. In a free economy, the volume of investment in a given period is determined by the 2.___
   A. demand for consumer goods and the volume of savings
   B. level of national income and the volume of money
   C. average return on investment and the volume of savings
   D. marginal efficiency of capital and the interest rate

3. The principle of comparative cost applies to 3.___
   A. pricing under conditions of imperfect competition
   B. determination of economic profit
   C. the analysis of marginal productivity
   D. analyses of international trade

4. The concept of the multiplier in economic analysis refers to the effect of 4.___
   A. increased demand on investment
   B. the interest rate on saving
   C. increased investment on income
   D. increased income on the propensity to consume

5. A significant increase in the liquidity preference will tend to have the effect of 5.___
   A. encouraging investment
   B. raising the interest rate
   C. increasing the marginal efficiency of capital
   D. reducing the supply of money

6. Which one of the following statements is INCORRECT with regard to holding companies? 6.___
   A. Holding companies are subject to more serious legal restrictions than are other forms of combination.
   B. Public utility holding companies above the second level are forbidden by federal law.

C. Holding companies allow companies in a combination to retain their separate identities.
D. Holding companies can exercise control over subsidiaries without outright ownership of their assets.

7. The statement, *Industry-wide collective bargaining tends to take wages and working conditions out of competition*, refers to the effect of such bargaining on the possibility of 7.___
A. sanctioning featherbedding in contracts
B. introducing new machinery and improved processes
C. reducing production costs for all employers
D. passing increased labor costs along to consumers

8. Which one of the following is NOT used in the computation of the gross national product? 8.___
A. Personal consumption expenditures
B. Gross private domestic investment
C. Income of unincorporated businesses
D. Government purchases of goods and services

9. Under a system of flexible farm price supports, 9.___
A. only the so-called *basic* commodities receive price support
B. price supports are applied when marketing quotas are inapplicable
C. acreage allotments, as a production control device, are abandoned
D. price support levels are fixed in relation to supply levels of products

10. Which one of the following economic problems will result when dollars pumped into the economy of an underdeveloped country are changed into local currency? 10.___
A. The effect will be inflationary unless compensated for by exports from that country.
B. Economic development will be curbed unless aid is offered on a grant rather than on a loan basis.
C. No real contribution to economic development will occur unless funds are employed in self-liquidating projects.
D. The effect will be inflationary unless accompanied by additional imports into that country.

11. Which one of the following pairs of economists is INCORRECTLY associated as having similar viewpoints on economic theory? 11.___
A. Edward Chamberlain - Joan Robinson
B. John Bates Clark - Wesley C. Mitchell
C. John R. Commons - Thorstein Veblen
D. William Stanley Jevons - Leon Walros

12. Which one of the following BEST expresses the theme of THE TWENTIETH CENTURY CAPITALIST REVOLUTION by Adolf A. Berle, Jr.? 12.___
   A. The present trend toward increased corporate influence in broad problems of community development must be reversed.
   B. The concept of the *soulless* corporation must be replaced by a concept of a corporate conscience.
   C. Means should be found to reduce the control exercised over the largest corporate units by the financial market.
   D. The absence of competition, in our present system of corporate concentrates, must be corrected.

13. Which author is INCORRECTLY linked with the book which he wrote? 13.___
   A. Henry George - PROGRESS AND POVERTY
   B. Gustavus Myers - FRENZIED FINANCE
   C. Frank Norris - THE OCTOPUS
   D. Norbert Wiener - THE HUMAN USE OF HUMAN BEINGS

14. Joan Robinson, Edward H. Chamberlin, and Robert Triffin are noted CHIEFLY for their contributions in the areas of 14.___
   A. monopolistic or imperfect competition
   B. money and banking
   C. international trade
   D. public and private finance

15. In which of the following items is the public policy NOT correctly associated with the name of the economist? 15.___
   A. Welfare state - John A. Hobson
   B. Laissez-faire - John Ruskin
   C. Labor legislation - John R. Commons
   D. Tariffs - Henry Carey

16. Henry Hazlett's ECONOMICS IN ONE LESSON is MOST accurately described as 16.___
   A. a socialist critique of capitalism
   B. non-Keynesian advocacy of laissez-faire
   C. criticism of ideas presented by the Keynesian school
   D. a popularization of Keynesian theory

17. Thorstein Veblen, to the extent that he could be said to be part of a group, was CLOSEST to which of the following? 17.___
   A. Max Weber, Somart, Schmoller
   B. Marshall, Pigou, Mill
   C. Von Wieser, Bohm-Bawerk, Menger
   D. Davenport, Patten, John Bates Clark

18. W.C. Mitchell, A.F. Burns, F.C. Mills, and Simon Kuznets were associated in the work of the 18.___
   A. Council of Economic Advisers
   B. National Bureau of Economic Research
   C. Committee for Economic Development
   D. Brookings Institution

19. The view of Karl Marx on the economic position of labor was that labor 19.___
   A. could not be considered a commodity
   B. was a commodity just like any other
   C. was a commodity of a unique type
   D. was sometimes a commodity and sometimes not, depending on the circumstances

20. Which of the following business cycle theorists is INCORRECTLY paired with a theory? 20.___
   A. W.S. Jevons - Sunspot theory
   B. J.M. Keynes - Savings-Investment theory
   C. J. Schumpeter - Innovation theory
   D. J.A. Hobson - Monetary theory

21. Marginalism in economics is MOST closely based on the psychology of 21.___
   A. Darwin B. Bentham C. Koffka D. James

22. The acceleration principle in the business cycle theory refers to the fact that 22.___
   A. the demand for productive agents fluctuates more sharply than does the demand for ultimate products
   B. unemployment spreads more rapidly as recession continues
   C. new investment will increase the total national income by more than the amount of the new investment
   D. inventories fluctuate more widely than does output

23. Which of the following are characteristics of monopolistic competition? 23.___
   I. Division of sales territory
   II. Product differentiation
   III. Price leadership
   IV. Relatively few producers
   V. Cartel agreements

   The CORRECT answer is:
   A. I, II, III B. I, IV, V
   C. II, III, IV D. III, V

24. A term which has come into frequent use in recent economic theory is *the multiplier*. 24.___
   This refers to the
   A. inflationary spiral
   B. relationship between oligopolistic industry and the price level
   C. relationship between changes in investment and consequent changes in consumption
   D. relationship between technological progress in an industry and the level of individual production

25. J. Kenneth Galbraith's reference to the so-called *countervailing force* in the American economy referred to the 25.___
A. rise of the C.I.O. in the 1930's and 40's that stimulated a phenomenal growth in the labor movement
B. trust-busting campaign of Theodore Roosevelt, stemming the growth towards bigness
C. passage of the Taft-Hartley Act, tilting the scales backward for the benefit of the employer
D. force, unleashed by the New Deal through its sympathy for labor, that brought about a redistribution of national income

KEY (CORRECT ANSWERS)

1. A
2. D
3. D
4. C
5. B

6. A
7. D
8. C
9. D
10. D

11. B
12. B
13. B
14. A
15. B

16. B
17. A
18. B
19. C
20. D

21. B
22. A
23. C
24. C
25. D

TEST 4

DIRECTIONS: Each question or incomplete statement is followed by several suggested answers or completions. Select the one that BEST answers the question or completes the statement. *PRINT THE LETTER OF THE CORRECT ANSWER IN THE SPACE AT THE RIGHT.*

1. The basing point system of fixing prices refers to the practice among producers in the same industry of charging 1.___
   A. the same price and adding freight charges from a common point, regardless of actual freight costs
   B. the same price and adding freight costs based on the average distance from all mills to the delivery point
   C. the F.O.B. price based on the average cost of production in all mills
   D. a competitive price and adding freight charges from a common point, regardless of actual freight costs

2. The characteristics of a free competitive market are BEST illustrated in the case of a(n) 2.___
   A. organized exchange
   B. well-advertised product
   C. large number of companies
   D. auction

3. The fact that Switzerland undersells the United States in watch movements in spite of the existence of equally skilled watchmakers is an illustration of the law of _____ costs. 3.___
   A. comparative
   B. diminishing
   C. absolute
   D. increasing

4. The effect of deficit financing by the federal government is to 4.___
   A. increase idle cash balances in the hands of the public
   B. increase unemployment in the short run
   C. increase the total amount of United States Notes outstanding
   D. maintain or increase the national income

5. In which of the following pairs did the second statute legalize acts previously prohibited by the first? 5.___
   I. Sherman Anti-Trust Act - Webb-Pomerene Act
   II. National Industrial Recovery Act - Public Utility Holding Company Act
   III. Norris-LaGuardia Anti-Injunction Act - National Labor Relations Act
   IV. Clayton Anti-Trust Act - Miller-Tydings Act

   The CORRECT answer is:
   A. I, IV
   B. II, IV
   C. I, II, III
   D. I, II, III, IV

6. The status of American agriculture during and after World War II differed MOST from that of the period of World War II in the 6.___
   A. reasons for the advance of agricultural prices
   B. extent of increase in farm mortgage debt
   C. changes in agriculture prices in the postwar years
   D. behavior of the foreign market for American farm products

7. Under flexible or variable price supports for farm commodities, the MAXIMUM support level would be approached when 7.___
   A. the ratio of total supplies to normal supplies fell
   B. the export market expanded
   C. overproduction increased
   D. marketing quotas were disapproved

8. To meet the problem of surplus commodities, states have attempted to overcome the constitutional prohibition on interstate tariffs by 8.___
   A. promoting a constitutional amendment
   B. utilizing their police powers
   C. advertising state specialities on a national scale
   D. passing legislation to curtail production

9. Unemployment is likely to be low if 9.___
   A. consumer demand remains stable
   B. employers grant wage increases as demanded by unions
   C. the price level drops gradually in response to increasing productivity
   D. no inflationary gap develops

10. MOST of the controversy in the courts in regard to utility rates has centered around 10.___
   A. what rate of profit is fair
   B. how the properties of a public utility should be valued
   C. how to determine the reasonableness of operating expenses
   D. the division of power between federal and state agencies

11. Which one of the following was a factor in the development of the other three? 11.___
   A. Growing surpluses of capital in the United States
   B. Tendency of producers of American staples to deal directly with foreign markets rather than through European brokers
   C. Change in the status of the United States from a debtor to a creditor nation
   D. Rise of New York as a rival of London as an international transactions center

12. Which of the following factors in the development of shipbuilding apply MORE to Great Britain than to the United States? 12.___
   A. Mass production of standardized ships
   B. Existence of rivers with wide, open estuaries
   C. Relative importance of foreign trade in the nation's economy
   D. Proximity to areas of steel production

13. Which one of the following statements is TRUE concerning the production of gold? 13.___
It(s)
   A. fluctuations in the past two decades have responded to changes in the legally established price
   B. has no influence on purchasing power of countries in international trade
   C. is a currently important factor in causing fluctuations in the price level in the United States
   D. is influenced by the fact that it is mined in close association with other metals

14. The McGuire Act increased the effectiveness of state *fair trade* laws as compared with their former status by 14.___
   A. adding liquor and drugs to the list of items in which fair trade contracts can be enforced
   B. making it possible to bind non-signers as well as signers of fair trade contracts
   C. adding interstate price-fixing agreements to the Miller-Tydings Law's provision for intrastate price fixing
   D. reaffirming the Supreme Court's 1950 decision as to the status of price-fixing agreements

15. Which of the following were characteristic of United States tariff legislation of the period 1934-1953? 15.___
   I. The abolition of the Tariff Commission
   II. The granting of greater tariff-making powers to the President
   III. The elimination of unconditional most-favored-nation clauses
   IV. The abandonment of the *Buy American* Act

The CORRECT answer is:
   A. II *only*
   B. I, II
   C. II, III
   D. III, IV

16. MOST of the loans made by the International Bank for Reconstruction and Development come from 16.___
   A. sale of its bonds
   B. its earnings
   C. funds raised from its parent body (the UN)
   D. assessments paid by member nations

17. Cost of production will have the GREATEST influence on the price of a commodity in the case of 17.___
   A. classical paintings in the hands of an art dealer
   B. fresh strawberries in a retail store
   C. antiques offered for sale at an exhibition
   D. shoes sold by a manufacturer

18. Monopolistic competition is 18.___
   A. a contradiction in terms
   B. cut-throat competition preliminary to the formation of complete monopoly
   C. competition among monopolized industries
   D. characterized by product differentiation in the same market

19. Which one of the following is NOT a characteristic of industries generally considered to be public utilities? 19.___
   A. The proportion of labor to material agents is large.
   B. They are frequently decreasing cost industries.
   C. There are usually no close substitutes.
   D. Duplication of service may lead to ineffiency or inconvenience to customers.

20. The *Pittsburgh plus* system of quoting steel prices was an example of 20.___
   A. monopsony
   B. the basing point principle
   C. agreement not to absorb freight charges
   D. assuring the same net prices to all steel mills

21. Which of the following government agencies is MOST concerned with granting direct subsidies to the industry involved? 21.___
   A. Maritime Commission
   B. Federal Communications Commission
   C. Interstate Commerce Commission
   D. Civil Aeronautics Authority

22. The CHIEF reason for the striking gains in American agricultural production during the past two decades has been the increase in 22.___
   A. total acreage B. productivity
   C. number of farm workers D. imports

23. The trend toward the abandonment of the one-crop system of agriculture in the southern states has led to 23.___
   A. an increase in the number of family-sized farms
   B. heavy migration of Black farm workers from the northern to the southern states
   C. relatively less reliance on federal price supports for the *basic* commodities
   D. substantial decline in the production of cotton

24. Which of the following trends is a result of the other three? 24.___
   A. Shift of population away from rural areas
   B. Increased mechanization of agriculture
   C. Depletion of soil fertility
   D. Improvement in general business conditions

25. Which one of the following groupings includes laws which were CLOSELY related to each other? 25.___
   A. Social Security Act, Wheeler-Rayburn Act, Fair Labor Standards Act
   B. National Labor Relations Act, Taft-Hartley Law, Webb-Pomerene Act
   C. Sherman Anti-trust Act, Clayton Act, Robinson-Patman Act
   D. Walsh-Healey Act, Federal Reserve Act, Glass-Steagall Act

---

KEY (CORRECT ANSWERS)

1. A
2. A
3. A
4. D
5. A

6. B
7. A
8. B
9. C
10. B

11. A
12. C
13. D
14. B
15. A

16. A
17. D
18. D
19. A
20. B

21. A
22. B
23. C
24. A
25. C

TEST 5

DIRECTIONS: Each question or incomplete statement is followed by several suggested answers or completions. Select the one that BEST answers the question or completes the statement. *PRINT THE LETTER OF THE CORRECT ANSWER IN THE SPACE AT THE RIGHT.*

1. Which one of the following objections to a steadily increasing public debt involves a fallacy? 1.___
   A. Fear of the debt may deter investment.
   B. Interest must be paid by taxes or further borrowing.
   C. Our generation is spared at the expense of future generations.
   D. Expenditure may be wasteful if no ceiling to the debt is enforced.

2. When a nation devalues its currency, the tendency is to 2.___
   A. increase imports
   B. decrease its tourist trade
   C. reduce its dollar shortage
   D. lower prices in Great Britain

3. Which one of the following is NOT a plan for alleviating the effects of the business cycle? 3.___
   A. The Social Credit Program
   B. The compensated dollar
   C. Pump priming
   D. The International Stabilization Fund

4. A law office purchases a new computer system and decides to take a depreciation deduction. The computer was purchased in January 1992. 4.___
   Which system of depreciation will be used?
   A. Straight Line Depreciation (SLD)
   B. Accelerated Cost Recovery System (ACRS)
   C. Modified Accelerated Cost Recovery System (MACRS)
   D. Real Property Cost Depreciation (RPD)

5. The idea of conspicuous consumption was FIRST set forth by 5.___
   A. Karl Marx
   B. Thorstein Veblen
   C. John Stuart Mill
   D. Wesley C. Mitchell

6. In the history of horizontal combinations for the purpose of eliminating competition, the form which developed LAST was the 6.___
   A. community of interest
   B. trust
   C. holding company
   D. pool

7. Which of the following would tend to cause inflation? Increase in 7.___
   I. the supply of gold
   II. production
   III. the supply of credit
   IV. the velocity of circulation of money

   The CORRECT answer is:
   A. I, II, III, IV
   B. II, III, IV
   C. I, III, IV
   D. II, IV

8. The corporate form of business organization is popular in small family enterprises because 8.___
   A. corporations decentralize management
   B. corporations are subject to less government regulation than individual entrepreneurs
   C. the tax rate for corporations is less than that of individual owners
   D. the corporation provides for limited liability

9. Which of the following will result from an increase in loans to businessmen by a bank? 9.___
   A
   I. rise in the deposits of the bank
   II. rise in the profits of the bank
   III. rise in the assets of the bank
   IV. decrease in the cash on hand of the bank

   The CORRECT answer is:
   A. I, II, IV
   B. I, III, IV
   C. I, II, III
   D. II, IV

10. Of the following, the one LEAST likely to affect consumption would be 10.___
    A. the expectation of changes in prices
    B. a change in the distribution of the national income
    C. the expectation of changes in supply
    D. changes in income tax rates for higher incomes

11. In general, statistics indicate MOST consistently that as the family income rises, the percentage of the income spent on 11.___
    A. food increases
    B. rent decreases
    C. food decreases
    D. luxuries decreases

12. Of the following, the one which is a RESULT of the other three is: 12.___
    A. Stockholders are numerous and scattered throughout the world
    B. Stockholders generally consider themselves as investors rather than active partners in a firm
    C. The large corporation is often controlled by minority stockholders
    D. Many corporations permit voting by proxy

13. The theory that wages tend to remain at a level which is barely sufficient to support a worker and his family is known as the _____ theory. 13.___
A. wages fund
B. marginal productivity
C. subsistence
D. commodity

14. Which of the following pairs does NOT contain an employee and an employer weapon or tactic? 14.___
A. Boycott - injunction
B. Check-off - blacklist
C. Open shop - lockout
D. Closed shop - yellow-dog contract

15. Which one of the following is LIKELY to result from the other three? 15.___
A. Increasing reserve requirements
B. Raising the re-discount rate
C. Contraction of bank credit
D. Sale of securities in the open market by Federal Reserve Banks

16. Anything becomes money when it 16.___
A. is backed by a bank
B. has general acceptability
C. has intrinsic value
D. is backed by precious metals

17. The term *national debt* means the 17.___
A. obligations-to-pay of the federal government
B. interest-bearing debt of the federal government
C. sum total of all federal, state, and local debts
D. sum of all public and private debts

18. The Federal Reserve System is owned 18.___
A. and controlled by private banks
B. by the government and controlled by private banks
C. and controlled by the government
D. by private banks with control divided between the government and representatives of the banks

19. Anti-trust laws have resulted in which of the following? 19.___
I. The dissolution of a majority of holding companies in America
II. The elimination of ruthless practices of great corporations.
III. The rise of a cartel system in the United States similar to that of Europe
IV. Government approval of reasonable combinations

The CORRECT answer is:
A. I, II, III
B. II, III, IV
C. I, II, III, IV
D. II, IV

20. Which of the following functions do the Federal Reserve Banks perform today? 20.___
I. Making loans
II. Issuing Federal Reserve Bank Notes
III. Creating their own credit
IV. Accepting deposits

The CORRECT answer is:
A. II, III
B. I, II, III
C. I, III, IV
D. I, II, IV

21. In recent years, the LARGEST proportion of the income of the federal government has been derived from _____ taxes. 21.___
A. corporation income
B. individual income
C. federal excise
D. estate and gift

22. Which of the following factors explain the failure of the cooperative movement in the United States to keep pace with the movement in other countries? 22.___
I. It has been marked by many conspicuous failures and bankruptcies.
II. Our marketing system is relatively more efficient than that of most countries.
III. The large geographical area of the country serves as a deterrent to cooperation.
IV. The individualistic character of the average American bodes no good for cooperation.

The CORRECT answer is:
A. I, II, III
B. II, III, IV
C. I, III
D. I, II, III, IV

23. Which one of the following does NOT tend to result from an overvalued currency? 23.___
A. Export and import prices in the overvalued domestic currencies are low.
B. The supplies available to the domestic economy are reduced.
C. The sale of goods abroad is discouraged.
D. Inflationary pressures are lessened.

24. Which one of the following does NOT correctly state a contrast between price competition and monopolistic competition? 24.___
A. In price competition, capital tends to be fully utilized whereas in monopolistic competition it is not.
B. Price competition usually results in wide price swings whereas, in monopolistic competition, there is usually price lethargy.
C. Price competition has cyclical price flexibility whereas monopolistic competition has little cyclical price flexibility.
D. In price competition, it usually pays the vendor to divert effort to selling and advertising whereas, in monopolistic competition, it does not.

25. Which of the following statements concerning pricing factors are TRUE? 25.___

I. When buyers feel that competing products are different, demand elasticities are lowered.
II. Where a low price is regarded as a sign of inferiority, the price elasticity of demand will be low.
III. Coordination of business policies in oligopolistic markets may exist without direct contacts among firms.
IV. Oligopoly is most often found in industries fabricating raw materials from farms.
V. The profitability in discrimination in pricing rests upon differences in the elasticities of demand of different groups.

The CORRECT answer is:
A. II, III, IV, V
B. I, III, V
C. I, II, III, V
D. I, II, IV

KEY (CORRECT ANSWERS)

1. C
2. C
3. D
4. B
5. B

6. C
7. C
8. D
9. C
10. D

11. C
12. C
13. C
14. C
15. C

16. B
17. B
18. D
19. D
20. C

21. B
22. B
23. B
24. D
25. C

EXAMINATION SECTION

TEST 1

DIRECTIONS: Each question or incomplete statement is followed by several suggested answers or completions. Select the one that BEST answers the question or completes the statement. *PRINT THE LETTER OF THE CORRECT ANSWER IN THE SPACE AT THE RIGHT.*

1. Economists who believe in the equilibrium theory of unemployment would be LEAST likely to place a major share of blame for unemployment on 1.___
   A. monetary conditions
   B. maldistribution of economic resources
   C. lack of mobility of labor
   D. government floors under prices and wages

2. Which one of the social functions listed below do interest and land rent perform? 2.___
   They
   A. act to withdraw resources from use in present consumption
   B. serve to direct their respective factors of production into the most valuable and useful channels
   C. stimulate increased supply of their respective factors
   D. help to maintain balance between the provision for present and future wants

3. Review of interest rates in specific countries over long periods of time reveals long-term trends of 3.___
   A. constancy, that can most reasonably be explained in terms of persistent traits of human psychology
   B. variability, that can be most correctly associated with changes in the productivity of capital
   C. variability, that can be most correctly associated with cyclical fluctuations in the economy
   D. constancy, that can most reasonably be explained in terms of consistent superiority of capitalistic methods of production over the techniques of less developed economies

4. Which of the following are CORRECT statements of modern economic theory as related to profit? 4.___
   I. Pure profit tends to disappear as a state of balanced competition is approached.
   II. Pure profit results from the imperfections of competition.
   III. Pure profit is the net income of a business as a whole, rather than the return for entrepreneurial service.
   IV. Scientific management and insurance have minimized the validity of the concept of profit as *compensation for risk-taking*.

The CORRECT answer is:
A. I, II, III, IV
B. I, II
C. III, IV
D. I, III

5. Study of United States corporate financing practices during the period after World War II indicates more financing by 5.___
A. bond issues than by stock issues, partly due to the tax advantage involved in bond financing
B. stock issues than by bond issues, partly due to the advantage involved in stock financing
C. stock issues than by bond issues, due to the shortage of equity capital
D. bond issues than by stock issues, due to the shortage of equity capital

6. Which one of the following statements concerning the control of monetary and credit conditions in the United States is NOT correct? 6.___
A. The fact that the Federal Reserve Board supported the government securities market during World War II and after, resulted in member banks becoming independent of Federal Reserve restraints.
B. The United States Treasury must work through the Federal Reserve System to effect its purposes in relation to money and credit supply.
C. Since the early 1920's, the Federal Reserve authorities have relied chiefly on open-market operations rather than rediscount rate changes as the method of credit control.
D. The policy of gold sterilization in the 1930's kept gold coming into the country from increasing the excess reserves then prevailing in the banks.

7. Which of the following statements are CORRECT concerning the settlement of labor disputes in the United States? 7.___
I. The Taft-Hartley Act prescribes conditions for reporting disputes to the Federal Mediation and Conciliation Service.
II. Agents of the Federal Mediation and Conciliation Service may act as mediators or arbitrators, depending upon the circumstances of the case.
III. If disputants agree to submit a dispute to arbitration by the Service, the decision is binding and refusal to abide by the award is punishable by criminal penalties.
IV. The National Railroad Adjustment Board and the National Mediation Board handle railway labor disputes.
V. The law establishing machinery for settling railway labor disputes forbids strikes on the railroads.

The CORRECT answer is:
A. I, II, IV
B. I, IV
C. II, III, V
D. I, III, IV

8. Under the national emergency provisions of the Labor Management Relations Act of 1947 (Taft-Hartley), 8.___
   A. mediation of the dispute may be ordered by the President of the United States
   B. seizure of affected plants by the federal government is authorized if Congress concurs
   C. the federal government may obtain an injunction delaying a strike for eighty days
   D. compulsory arbitration may be invoked by the President

9. Which one of the following pairs is matched INCORRECTLY? 9.___
   A. Constant dollars - Price indexes
   B. Auto licenses - *Ability to pay* principle of taxation
   C. Net national product - Gross national product minus depreciation
   D. Secular stagnation - Keynes-Hansen thesis

10. The BASIC purpose of our federal and state conservation programs has been to 10.___
   A. preserve our natural resources for the purpose of ultimately deriving an important source of income for the federal budget
   B. aid the consumer by increasing the production of consumer goods and thus reducing prices
   C. help make our internal waterways, our forests, and our watersheds self-supporting and thus reduce the burden on government
   D. protect the public interest against treatment of our natural resources solely as sources of immediate income and not as capital assets

11. If the names Joseph A. Schumpeter, Wesley C. Mitchell, and A.F. Burns were mentioned in a discussion, the subject matter under discussion would be MOST likely that of 11.___
   A. money and banking
   B. business cycles
   C. housing
   D. social security

12. One of the MAJOR economic characteristics of the United States in the 1920's was a(n) 12.___
   A. low national income
   B. high degree of unemployment
   C. growing concentration of the control of industry
   D. increasing proportionate distribution of our national wealth among farmers, workers, and businessmen

13. Which one of the following aspects of the government's farm program has resulted in government ownership of large stocks of agricultural products? 13.___
   A. Nonrecourse loans
   B. *Soil bank* payments
   C. Export subsidies
   D. National School Lunch Program

14. An economist known for supporting the idea that some inflation is NOT necessarily an economic evil is 14.___
   A. Marcus Nadler B. G. Rowland Collins
   C. Paul A. Samuelson D. Sumner H. Slichter

15. Which one of the following is TRUE with regard to the consumer cooperative movement? 15.___
   A. The number of shares which one may buy is usually unlimited.
   B. Only members may purchase goods from the cooperative.
   C. All members of a consumer's cooperative have equal voting rights.
   D. An annual dividend based on profits is paid on each share.

16. Which one of the following was MOST unlike the other three in his social and political outlook? 16.___
   A. Robert Owen B. Mikhail Bakunin
   C. Louis Blanc D. Charles Fourier

17. The concept of the *economic man* in the history of economic thought relates to an individual who seeks to 17.___
   A. further his economic self-interest above anything else
   B. create a balance and equilibrium among the factors of consumption, production, distribution, and exchange
   C. make the superiority of capitalism over socialism a reality
   D. interpret politics mainly in the light of economic factors

18. According to the law of monopoly price, a monopolist will charge that price which will give him the 18.___
   A. greatest net profit
   B. highest price that consumers are willing to pay
   C. lowest cost of production
   D. greatest number of sales of his product

19. During the first decade of the 20th century, the American farmer enjoyed a period of comparatively sustained prosperity despite the fact that 19.___
   A. the number of his domestic competitors was increasing
   B. he was rapidly losing a large part of his foreign market
   C. his political influence was waning
   D. there was a deflationary movement after the discovery of gold in the Yukon

20. Unemployment which occurs when workers move from job to job is known as _____ unemployment. 20.___
   A. frictional B. seasonal
   C. technological D. cyclical

21. Which one of the following is INCORRECTLY matched? 21.___
   A. Joan Robinson - Imperfect Competition
   B. Edward H. Chamberlin - Monopolistic Competition
   C. Thorstein Veblen - Institutional Economics
   D. Francis A. Walker - Welfare Economics

22. According to the theories of J.M. Keynes, which one of the following factors is LEAST important in determining the level of employment and national income? 22.___
   A. Liquidity preference
   B. Wage bargaining between employers and employees
   C. The propensity to consume
   D. The marginal efficiency of capital

23. Which one of the following is NOT true concerning the various forms of business enterprise? 23.___
   A. Although approximately one-half of all manufacturing businesses in the United States are operated by single entrepreneurs, they account for only approximately ten percent of the manufactured output.
   B. Convertible bonds are those bonds which may be converted into income bonds on which interest is payable only if there are earnings by the corporation.
   C. Some securities are exempted from *blue-sky* laws because they are listed upon recognized stock exchanges.
   D. Some states have acted to help partnerships by laws permitting some limitation on the liability of the members.

24. Buying and selling the same commodity at the same time, but in two different markets, to take advantage of differences in the price of the commodity in the two places at the same instant, is known as 24.___
   A. hedging
   B. a joint operational cost
   C. arbitrage
   D. an open market operation

25. Which one of the following is NOT true concerning the control of credit by the federal government? 25.___
The
   A. Securities and Exchange Commission can raise or lower margin requirements on stock sales
   B. Federal Reserve Board places certain restrictions on bank loans on real estate
   C. Federal Reserve Board may raise or lower the rediscount rate
   D. Federal Reserve Board does not control consumer credit at present

KEY (CORRECT ANSWERS)

1. A
2. B
3. A
4. A
5. A

6. B
7. A
8. C
9. B
10. D

11. B
12. C
13. A
14. D
15. C

16. B
17. A
18. A
19. B
20. A

21. D
22. B
23. B
24. C
25. A

TEST 2

DIRECTIONS: Each question or incomplete statement is followed by several suggested answers or completions. Select the one that BEST answers the question or completes the statement. *PRINT THE LETTER OF THE CORRECT ANSWER IN THE SPACE AT THE RIGHT.*

1. In the course of production of goods by the modern corporation, marginal costs are those costs which 1.___
   A. are considered variable costs
   B. are considered fixed costs
   C. result from a one-unit addition to output
   D. are obtained by dividing the total cost of production by the number of units produced

2. The OPTIMUM economic situation in regard to population in any country is 2.___
   A. that number of people whose labor will produce the largest possible per capita product
   B. the greatest number of people that country has ever had
   C. that time in a country's history of population where there has been developed the highest per capita income
   D. one in which there is a balance between industrial and agricultural workers

3. With which one of the following is the *iron law of wages* MOST closely associated? 3.___
   A. David Ricardo
   B. Leon Walras
   C. Adam Smith
   D. Alfred Marshall

4. A school of economic thought which had as its central doctrine the idea of the *net surplus* or the *product-net* was the 4.___
   A. physiocratic
   B. classical
   C. institutional
   D. mathematical

5. Which one of the following is a CORRECT statement in regard to the Federal Deposit Insurance Corporation? 5.___
   A. Insurance of bank deposits was included in the original Federal Reserve Act.
   B. The insurance maximum is currently $100,000 on each individual.
   C. The F.D.I.C. obtains its funds from government appropriations.
   D. All banks which have savings accounts are automatically eligible for F.D.I.C. protection.

6. Which one of the following statements concerning elasticity of demand in a system of private enterprise is TRUE? 6.___
   A. The demand for the product of each firm is elastic in a perfectly competitive industry.
   B. Demand becomes inelastic in a completely monopolistic situation.
   C. Elasticity of demand is increased when some firms in an industry obtain strong consumer preference.
   D. Elasticity of demand is increased in an imperfectly competitive industry.

7. Which one of the following is NOT a provision of the Taft-Hartley Law? 7.___
   A. Unions engaging in strikes or other activities which violate contracts with employers are subject to damage suits in the federal courts.
   B. Both prosecuting and judicial functions in administering the Taft-Hartley Law are combined in the NLRB.
   C. At least sixty days notice must be given by unions and employers before existing contracts may be modified or terminated.
   D. Featherbedding is included among labor practices prohibited by law.

8. Which one of the following is LEAST speculative in its operations? 8.___
   _____ transactions.
   A. Bear   B. Bull
   C. Bucket shop   D. Hedging

9. Which one of the following abuses in the public utility field did NOT lead to the passage of the Wheeler-Rayburn Act? 9.___
   A. Pyramided holding companies
   B. Issuance of watered stock
   C. *Milking* and *padding*
   D. Monopoly

10. A long term capital gain or loss occurs when the capital asset involved in the transaction is held 10.___
   A. six months or longer
   B. one year or longer
   C. eight months or longer
   D. eighteen months or longer

11. The term *dollar gap* is used in economic literature PRIMARILY in discussions of 11.___
   A. the federal budget
   B. international trade balances
   C. foreign exchange rates
   D. personal savings ratios

12. The doctrine of comparative costs is the underlying basis for the principle of 12.___
    A. protectionism
    B. mercantilism
    C. free trade
    D. colonialism

13. In which group do ALL of the items represent an enumeration of a corporation's working capital? 13.___
    A. Bank deposits, patent rights, franchises
    B. Finished products on hand, deposits in banks, accounts receivable
    C. Patent rights, franchises, raw materials on hand
    D. Deposits in banks, lands and buildings, machinery

14. Which one of the following is NOT a function of the Board of Governors of the Federal Reserve System? 14.___
    A. The determination of margin requirements for stock purchases
    B. The determination of the general monetary, credit, and operating policies of the Federal Reserve System
    C. The right to *review and determine* the rediscount rates
    D. The issuance of Federal Reserve notes

15. With which of the following areas of improvement was Frederick W. Taylor MOST concerned in his studies on scientific management? 15.___
    The
    A. handling of inventories, deliveries, and accounting practices
    B. improvement of welfare benefits through labor-management conferences
    C. performance of the individual worker at the individual's workplace
    D. performance of management

16. Which of the following governmental actions tend to aggravate inequality of income? 16.___
    I. Taxes on corporate profits
    II. Social Security payments
    III. Paying interest on the public debt
    IV. Sales taxes

    The CORRECT answer is:
    A. I, IV B. III, IV C. I, II D. II, III

17. Which of the following forms of income is INCORRECTLY associated with its meaning? 17.___
    I. Disposable income - The total income earned by a worker
    II. Unearned income - Income received from returns on investments
    III. Real income - Amount of goods and services that can be bought for a dollar
    IV. Psychic income - Satisfaction derived by a doctor from owning a famous oil painting

The CORRECT answer is:
A. I, III B. II *only* C. II, IV D. I *only*

18. Which one of the following was NOT a function of the United States Housing Authority? 18.___
A. Insure against losses from mortgages held on real estate
B. Grant aid for slum clearance
C. Help in the building of low rent housing
D. Grant loans to local public housing agencies

19. Which of the following functions did the Commodity Credit Corporation NOT exercise? 19.___
A. Dispose of some surplus farm products through non-commercial channels
B. Make loans on farm products to participating producers
C. Buy some farm products to support their prices on the market
D. Make direct payments to producers of perishable farm products sold at free market prices

20. Which one of the following statements about the TVA is NOT correct? 20.___
A. Funds for expansion of its power plants are obtained from the sale of bonds.
B. It uses its receipts from the sale of power to conduct its power business.
C. Part of its activities is financed by annual appropriations of Congress.
D. Atomic energy plants are among its largest customers.

21. Which of the following were provided for in the Wheeler-Lea Act of 1938? 21.___
I. The FTC could act directly on its own initiative to suppress unfair business practices.
II. It provided sufficient funds to permit the FTC to do an effective job in protecting consumers.
III. It applied only to commodities sold in interstate trade or advertised across state lines.
IV. The FTC could penalize advertisers only after appropriate court action had been successful.

The CORRECT answer is:
A. I, III B. II, IV C. I, II D. III, IV

22. The purpose of the Miller-Tydings Act was to 22.___
A. prevent the setting of monopoly prices by manufacturers
B. prevent large chains from driving small retailers out of business
C. prevent too great a spread between wholesale and retail prices
D. encourage competition at the retail level

23. Which of the following are characteristic of a consumer cooperative that has adopted the Rochdale form of organization? 23.___
   I. If a profit is made, consumer-members may receive patronage dividends.
   II. Consumer-members may purchase their necessities both on a cash and credit basis.
   III. In order to ensure a democratic control, each member in the cooperative is given a maximum of one vote.
   IV. The rate of interest on shares varies with cooperative earnings.

   The CORRECT answer is:
   A. I, III B. I, II C. II, IV D. III, IV

24. Which of the following pairs presents a significant contrast in terms of labor gains in the United States? 24.___
   A. Commonwealth v. Hunt, 1842 - National Labor Relations Act, 1935
   B. Clayton Act, 1914 - Adamson Act, 1916
   C. Danbury Hatters Case, 1908 - National Recovery Act, 1933
   D. Seamen's Act, 1916 - Fair Labor Standards Act, 1938

25. Which of the following provisions is NOT contained in the Taft-Hartley Act? 25.___
   A. Providing for a reconstruction of the NLRB
   B. Broadening the legal rights of employers
   C. Increasing the responsibility of labor unions
   D. Outlawing the union shop and maintenance of membership classes

---

KEY (CORRECT ANSWERS)

1. C
2. A
3. A
4. A
5. B

6. A
7. B
8. D
9. D
10. B

11. B
12. C
13. B
14. D
15. C

16. B
17. D
18. A
19. D
20. A

21. A
22. B
23. A
24. C
25. D

TEST 3

DIRECTIONS: Each question or incomplete statement is followed by several suggested answers or completions. Select the one that BEST answers the question or completes the statement. *PRINT THE LETTER OF THE CORRECT ANSWER IN THE SPACE AT THE RIGHT.*

1. Which of the following statements are CORRECT as regards the Malthusian theory? 1.___
   I. As population increases, food supply will increase proportionally.
   II. Population increases in geometric ratio, while food supply increases in arithmetic ratio.
   III. Population, unless curbed by natural and other forces, tends to outrun food supply.
   IV. Conditions in highly industrialized countries have challenged the general applicability of the Malthusian theory.

   The CORRECT answer is:
   A. I, II B. II, III, IV
   C. I, II, IV D. III, IV, I

2. Which of the following statements are attributable to Karl Marx? 2.___
   I. A preceding generation cannot bind a succeeding one by its laws or controls.
   II. The history of all hitherto existing societies is the history of class struggle.
   III. This country with its institutions belongs to the people who inhabit it.
   IV. Workingmen of all countries unite.

   The CORRECT answer is:
   A. I, II B. II, IV C. I, III D. III, IV

3. Which statement does NOT correctly characterize the reasons for the deep and prevailing dissatisfaction of institutional economists with neo-classical economic doctrines? 3.___
   A. Marshallian economics does not come to grips with present-day problems.
   B. Neo-classicism is but a refurbishing of generalizations made a century and more ago by the classicists in defense of the then ruling English classes.
   C. Institutionalists emphasize individual behavior along with value and price.
   D. Institutionalists' chief interest is in man-made institutions.

4. Which of the following statements regarding the *single tax* theory of Henry George are TRUE? 4.___
   I. It rests on the assumption that individual human labor constitutes the only justifiable title to property.
   II. His social philosophy is based on the fundamental distinction between land and capital.
   III. The application would be difficult since it necessitates separating the value of the land from the value of its improvements.
   IV. The modern single tax movement has done much to pave the way for a more equitable distribution of taxation.

   The CORRECT answer is:
   A. I, II, III, IV
   B. I, III
   C. I, II, IV
   D. III, IV

5. Which one of these ideas was NOT expressed by Adam Smith in THE WEALTH OF NATIONS? 5.___
   A. The recurrence of business cycles
   B. The principle of free trade
   C. The principle of free competition
   D. A nation's wealth consists of more than gold and silver

6. Which one of the following economists can be LEAST properly grouped with the other three? 6.___
   A. William Stanley Jevons
   B. Leon Walras
   C. Francois Quesnay
   D. Vilfredo Pareto

7. Which one of the following economists advanced the theory that an increase in wages to workers would result in improved standards which would, in turn, beget larger families, increase the labor supply, and, thus, force wages down? 7.___
   A. David Ricardo
   B. Charles Fourier
   C. Robert Owen
   D. Frederick Bastiat

8. Which one of the following is NOT one of the advantages of a corporation as a form of business organization? 8.___
   A. It insures a continuity of existence regardless of the life span of individuals.
   B. It makes possible the amassing of large amounts of capital in one business.
   C. Stockholders are relieved of all liability for losses in case of business failure.
   D. It affords the business certain privileges and immunities of a person before the law.

9. Which of the following was NOT a reason for the passage of the Gold Standard Act of 1900? 9.___
   A. Fresh gold deposits had been recently discovered in Alaska, Australia, and South Africa, assuring an adequate supply for the backing of paper currency

B. The quantity of paper currency in circulation was shrinking because the public refused to buy bonds to finance the Spanish-American War.
C. The victory of the Republican Party in the election was viewed as a rejection of bimetallism.
D. The farmer was enjoying a temporary prosperity brought on by foreign crop failures.

10. Which of the following is an INCORRECT application of the *safety valve* theory of agriculture and the frontier as it affected labor? 10.___
A. There is little evidence that the existence of cheap lands operated in any effective fashion to raise wages of industrial labor.
B. Throughout the period of industrialism, the movement of population from the country to the city had been greater than the movement from the city to the country.
C. The frontier did attract millions of immigrants and discontented townsmen from East and South who might have been forced into the ranks of industrial labor.
D. The *new* immigrants from Eastern and Southern Europe, by settling in large numbers in the West, had little influence on industrial labor.

11. Which of the following BEST illustrates the United States' withdrawal from economic isolation? 11.___
The
A. Johnson Debt Default Act of 1934
B. Hawley-Smoot Tariff Act of 1930
C. Reciprocal Trade Agreements Act of 1934
D. Neutrality Acts of 1935-37

12. The function of the International Monetary Fund is to 12.___
A. provide loans to backward nations for industrial development
B. stabilize national currencies
C. make loans for foreign trade
D. serve as a clearing house for reparation

13. Which one of the following statements BEST describes the relation of the NRA of 1933 to the Sherman Act of 1890 and the Clayton Act of 1914? 13.___
The NRA
A. was the first to provide penalties for the creation of combinations in restraint of trade
B. restated the *open shop* principles first formulated in the Sherman Act
C. suspended the earlier anti-trust laws
D. applied anti-trust measures to public utilities which were exempt under the earlier acts

14. Which of the following is a function of the Securities Exchange Commission? It 14.___
   A. sets margin requirements
   B. regulates prices on commodity exchanges
   C. registers securities sold in interstate commerce
   D. sets maximum rates charged by public utilities other than railroads

15. In which of the following pairs does the SECOND item represent a halt or reversal in legislation direction of the FIRST? 15.___
   A. Interstate Commerce Act - Hepburn Act
   B. Sherman Act - Clayton Act
   C. Norris-LaGuardia Act - Taft-Hartley Act
   D. Pure Food and Drugs Act - Wheeler-Lea Act

16. The statistical measure that shows the production of the country in terms of expenditures for goods and services is the 16.___
   A. index of commodity prices
   B. index of business activity
   C. cost-of-living index
   D. gross national product

17. President Clinton's stated policy concerning the government's farm program revealed opposition to _____ price supports. 17.___
   A. reciprocal
   B. rigid
   C. any type of
   D. flexible

18. The CHIEF reason as to why indirect taxes do not meet the principles of good taxation is that they 18.___
   A. cost too much to collect
   B. are too easy to evade
   C. are too annoying for the taxpayer
   D. are regressive

19. To determine the yield he will receive from a government bond, the investor should consider the _____ the bond. 19.___
   A. interest rate on
   B. face value and interest rate of
   C. price he pays for it and interest rate of
   D. maturity date and interest rate of

20. Which of the following are ESSENTIAL characteristics of a gold standard? 20.___
   I. The money unit is a definite weight and fineness of gold.
   II. There is convertibility of all other forms of money into gold.
   III. There is free and unlimited coinage of gold.
   IV. There is a restricted gold market with other countries.
   V. Gold is legal tender.

The CORRECT answer is:
A. I, II, III, IV
B. I, II, III, V
C. II, III, IV, V
D. I, IV, V

21. The MOST significant difference between demand deposits and time deposits in business practice today is that 21.___
A. advance notice is required before demand deposits may be withdrawn
B. separate banks must be used to maintain each of the two kinds of deposits
C. demand deposits do not earn interest
D. only time deposits may be insured by the F.D.I.C.

22. Basic to the understanding of our modern industrial society is the concept that saving and investment are 22.___
A. generally done by different people for different reasons
B. synonymous terms
C. generally done by the same people for a variety of reasons
D. always equal

23. Which of the following statements regarding commercial banks are TRUE? 23.___
I. Their loans create deposits.
II. Most of their loans are for short terms.
III. Their loans are primarily for the purpose of furthering profitable business enterprises.
IV. They do not pay interest on commercial deposits.

The CORRECT answer is:
A. I, II
B. III, IV
C. I, II, IV
D. I, II, III, IV

24. The power to fix margin requirements for trading in stocks is based upon authority granted in the 24.___
A. Securities Exchange Act
B. Federal Trade Commission Act
C. Federal Reserve Act
D. Federal Deposit Insurance Corporation Law

25. Which one of the following statements concerning the Norris-LaGuardia Act and its provisions is NOT true? 25.___
A. It was passed during the Hoover Administration.
B. Contracts under which employees agreed not to join free unions were enforceable only in federal courts.
C. An injunction could be issued only after a hearing in open court with both parties present.
D. Labor's right to organize should be protected by the United States government.

KEY (CORRECT ANSWERS)

1. B		11. C
2. B		12. B
3. C		13. C
4. A		14. C
5. A		15. C
6. C		16. D
7. A		17. B
8. C		18. D
9. B		19. C
10. D		20. B
	21. C	
	22. A	
	23. D	
	24. A	
	25. B	

TEST 4

DIRECTIONS: Each question or incomplete statement is followed by several suggested answers or completions. Select the one that BEST answers the question or completes the statement. *PRINT THE LETTER OF THE CORRECT ANSWER IN THE SPACE AT THE RIGHT.*

1. Which one of the following is NOT an aspect of our federal social security system? 1.___
   A. Retirement payments to wives of insured workers collecting benefits
   B. Payments to insured workers temporarily not working because of disability
   C. Payments for surviving dependent children of insured workers
   D. Lump-sum payments on death of insured workers

2. Which of the following statements regarding the Taft-Hartley Act are TRUE? 2.___
   I. All newly hired workers must join a union within a given period of time.
   II. Secondary boycotts are outlawed.
   III. A union may be sued for damages if it violates a contract.
   IV. Jurisdictional disputes are illegal.
   V. Employers may apply for injunctions to prevent a strike where the national welfare is involved.

   The CORRECT answer is:
   A. I, II, III, IV, V
   B. II, III, IV
   C. III, IV, I, II
   D. III, IV, II, V

3. As a result of the Employment Act of 1946, there is at present a 3.___
   A. standby program of public works
   B. federal unemployment insurance program
   C. federal employment service
   D. council of economic advisers

4. According to Gresham's Law, under bimetallism, the metal which will be driven out of circulation is 4.___
   A. more expensive per ounce in the open market
   B. more expensive per ounce in the mint
   C. valued at a lower ratio by the mint than in the market
   D. valued at a higher ratio by the mint than in the market

5. Which of the following would be APPROPRIATE illustrations of the basic principles of capital formation? 5.___
   I. A steel worker signs up for payroll deductions under his company's stock purchase plan
   II. A farmer buys a tractor instead of a sedan
   III. A corporation *passes a dividend* at the end of a profitable year
   IV. A bank's use of savings deposits to purchase railroad bonds

   The CORRECT answer is:
   A. I, III, IV
   B. I, II, IV
   C. II, III, IV
   D. I, II, III, IV

6. Which of the following dynamic forces or trends would exert a depressing or elevating effect on normal price? 6.___
   I. Increase of population
   II. Monetary disturbances
   III. Increase in real wages
   IV. Rise in the per unit expense of marketing

   The CORRECT answer is:
   A. I, II, III
   B. I, II, III, IV
   C. III, IV, I
   D. II, III, IV

7. Economists today GENERALLY agree that the equilibrium level of national income _____ the level of full employment of resources. 7.___
   A. may be above
   B. may be below
   C. must be above
   D. must be below

8. Which does NOT help to create a favorable balance of trade for a nation? 8.___
   A. *Blocked currency*
   B. Devaluation of currency
   C. Export licensing
   D. Payment of dividends by foreign firms

9. Though they are industrial giants, none of the Big Three automobile companies makes its own paint and finishes and only one makes its own steel. 9.___
   This illustration is MOST directly pertinent to a discussion of
   A. factors affecting industrial concentration
   B. basing point pricing and monopoly
   C. geographic division of labor
   D. disadvantages of the corporation

10. Which one of the following would be LEAST satisfactory as an explanation of a period of decline in the business cycle? 10.___
    A. Profitability of introduction of new capital goods starts to fall
    B. Planned savings fail to equal planned investment
    C. Volume of saving increases in relation to rate of consumption
    D. Tendency for costs to rise in a period of expansion

11. In teaching the problem of causes of inflation, emphasis should be placed on the relationship between 11.___
   A. purchasing power and demand for goods
   B. quantity of money and demand for goods
   C. purchasing power and supply of goods
   D. quantity of money and price level

12. A teacher uses this illustration: 30 minutes of a United States textile machine operator's time are needed to buy a pound of coffee. 12.___
The class is PROBABLY discussing
   A. price fixing
   B. variable costs
   C. international trade
   D. diminishing returns

13. Which one of the following economists does NOT belong in the same classification with the other three? 13.___
   A. Alfred Marshall
   B. Wesley C. Mitchell
   C. John R. Commons
   D. Thorstein Veblen

14. With which of the following is Thorstein Veblen LEAST properly associated? 14.___
   A. The Institutional School
   B. *The Theory of the Leisure Class*
   C. The defense of *the economic man*
   D. The concept of *conspicuous consumption*

15. Which one of the following does NOT belong in a list of *scientific socialists*? 15.___
   A. Karl Marx
   B. Robert Owen
   C. Friedrich Engels
   D. Carl Rodbertus

16. Which of the following economists is NOT generally associated with the *wages fund theory*? 16.___
   A. Nassau William Senior
   B. Thomas Malthus
   C. William S. Jevons
   D. James Mill

17. Which one of the following books deals PRIMARILY with the problem of secular trends rather than short-term fluctuations in national income? 17.___
   A. Burns & Mitchell - MEASURING BUSINESS CYCLES
   B. Von Haberler - PROSPERITY AND DEPRESSION
   C. Estey - BUSINESS CYCLE THEORY
   D. Hansen - FULL RECOVERY OR STAGNATION

18. Buying and selling at the same time, the one transaction being in the actual present market and the other in the future speculative market, is called 18.___
   A. selling short
   B. manipulation
   C. arbitrage
   D. hedging

19. The MAIN contention in favor of Henry George's SINGLE TAX is that 19.___
   A. economic rent is a social product
   B. it is based on ability to pay
   C. its cost of collection is low
   D. it directs use of land into socially beneficial fields

20. The objection of business to the demands of labor for a guaranteed annual wage are based on the facts that 20.___
I. the labor force would tend to lose mobility
II. new industries would have difficulty in finding employees
III. labor turnover would increase
IV. it would be more difficult to make price cuts to meet competition

The CORRECT answer is:
A. I, III
B. I, II, III, IV
C. II, IV
D. I, II, IV

21. Comparing the percentage rise in the general price level during World War I with that during World War II, it is MOST accurate to state that 21.___
A. there was little difference in the percentage rise
B. prices rose more rapidly during World War II
C. prices rose more rapidly during World War I
D. there is no method of making a statistical evaluation

22. The emphasis of the New Deal on *pump priming* indicated reliance on the monetary philosophy of 22.___
A. Alfred Marshall
B. Wesley C. Mitchell
C. J.M. Keynes
D. Simon Kuznets

23. Which of the following situations are the effects of a large volume of public debt? 23.___
I. Increased dependency of nation's banks on Treasury policy
II. Increased inflationary pressures
III. Increased efficiency of the tax structure
IV. Expansion of the tax system into new areas

The CORRECT answer is:
A. I, II, IV
B. I, II, III, IV
C. I, II
D. III, IV

24. The economic factors which may determine the quantity of money and credit in circulation are 24.___
I. the form in which the public wishes to hold its liquid assets
II. deficit financing by the United States government
III. an increase in loans by commercial banks
IV. importation of gold

The CORRECT answer is:
A. I, III, IV
B. III, IV
C. I, II
D. I, II, III, IV

25. Which of the following may back Federal Reserve notes? 25.___
I. Gold certificates
II. Commercial paper
III. Government securities
IV. Treasury notes of 1890

The CORRECT answer is:
A. I, II, III
B. II, III, IV
C. II, IV
D. I, III

KEY (CORRECT ANSWERS)

1. B
2. B
3. D
4. C
5. D

6. B
7. B
8. C
9. A
10. B

11. C
12. C
13. A
14. C
15. B

16. C
17. D
18. D
19. A
20. D

21. C
22. C
23. A
24. D
25. A

TEST 5

DIRECTIONS: Each question or incomplete statement is followed by several suggested answers or completions. Select the one that BEST answers the question or completes the statement. *PRINT THE LETTER OF THE CORRECT ANSWER IN THE SPACE AT THE RIGHT.*

1. The MAIN controls of the Federal Reserve System over the supply of money and credit are weakened when 1.___
   A. excess reserves of member banks increase
   B. the President suspends their use by Executive Order
   C. the Federal Reserve System raises the rediscount rate
   D. the Federal Reserve Bank conducts an open market operation

2. The establishment of which of the following resulted from an agreement arrived at by the international conference at Bretton Woods in 1944? 2.___
   I. International Monetary Fund
   II. International Bank for Reconstruction and Development
   III. International Trade Organization
   IV. European Recovery Plan

   The CORRECT answer is:
   A. I, II, III B. I, II
   C. II, III D. I, III, IV

3. Thorstein Veblen's theory that the modern economic system creates two types of values, economic and pecuniary, resulted in his conclusion that there is a basic difference between 3.___
   A. capital and labor
   B. industry and business
   C. government and the consumer
   D. trade and industrial unions

4. Which of the following statements CORRECTLY characterize American agriculture during the decade 1923-1932? 4.___
   I. Federal legislation was passed with a view to stabilizing the supply of farm products.
   II. With 1909-1914 as a base, farm prices were above parity during the first half and fell below parity during the second half of the period.
   III. The proportion of agricultural supplement to total employment declined.
   IV. The number of farms remained fairly constant.

   The CORRECT answer is:
   A. I, II, IV B. I, II, III
   C. II, III, IV D. I, III, IV

5. The situation in which a worker need NOT be a union member to be hired but must become and remain a union member to continue to be employed is known as a 5.___
A. union shop B. closed shop
C. open shop D. open union

6. Berle and Means, in THE MODERN CORPORATION AND PRIVATE PROPERTY, conclude that corporate control lies in the hands of 6.___
A. the majority of stockholders
B. investment banks
C. those who have actual power to select the Board of Directors
D. the largest investors in the corporation

7. Farm cooperatives are exempt from the provisions of the anti-trust laws as a result of the _____ Act. 7.___
A. Webb-Pomerene B. Capper-Volstead
C. Robinson-Patman D. Anderson

8. The American economist MOST closely associated with the study of business cycles is 8.___
A. John R. Commons B. Wesley C. Mitchell
C. Selig Perlman D. John Bates Clark

9. Which one of the following may CORRECTLY be considered the result of the other three? 9.___
A. Legislation in the state of Wisconsin
B. Social Security Act
C. Townsend Plan
D. Report of the Brookings Institution

10. Of the following items, the one with the LOWEST degree of elastic demand is 10.___
A. sirloin steak B. beef
C. food D. meat

11. The Randall Commission recommended 11.___
A. higher protective tariffs
B. a Buy-American program
C. the extension of reciprocal tariffs
D. the removal of tariffs

12. All of the following factors may account for the strengthening of the British pound EXCEPT 12.___
A. decreased imports of gold
B. increased British exports
C. decreased imports from the dollar area
D. lifting of wartime restrictions on exchange rates

13. A function of the International Monetary Fund is to 13.___
A. grant loans of a self-liquidating nature to under-developed countries
B. provide stability in foreign exchange rates while allowing freedom of action in coping with domestic problems

C. grant loans for relief and rehabilitation to members of the United Nations who sustained extensive damage during World War II
D. prevent the flight of capital from countries with unstable currencies

14. A number of chain stores receiving rebates from manufacturers have been prosecuted in violation of the ____ Act. 14.___
A. Miller-Tydings
B. Wheeler-Rayburn
C. Copeland-Lea
D. Robinson-Patman

15. A 6% sales tax on EVERY purchase of ANY kind would be, in effect, 15.___
A. proportional
B. inelastic
C. progressive
D. regressive

16. Which one of the following is NOT a device for achieving minority control of corporations? 16.___
A. The holding company
B. Non-voting stock
C. The voting trust
D. The joint-stock company

17. Which of the following ACCURATELY contrasts a corporation and a consumers' cooperative? 17.___
A. One vote per share; one vote per member
B. Chartered by the state; no charter of incorporation
C. Profits paid out as dividends; profits eliminated by charging low prices
D. Issue stock; no stock issued

18. The capital of a corporation is represented by $400,000 of 5% bonds and $200,000 of common stock. The corporation goes into bankruptcy, and its assets yield $100,000. The amount so realized is distributed as follows: _____ to bondholders, _____ to stockholders. 18.___
A. $80,000; $20,000
B. nothing; $100,000
C. $50,000; $50,000
D. $100,000; nothing

19. In the following paired items, the pair that contains examples of items from the two sides of a balance sheet is 19.___
A. inventory and good will
B. accounts receivable and surplus
C. notes payable and capital stock
D. cash and operating expenses

20. The International Ladies Garment Workers Union is a(n) 20.___
I. industrial union
II. vertical union
III. affiliated with the C.I.O.
IV. independent union

The CORRECT answer is:
A. I, II
B. I, II, III
C. I, III, IV
D. II, III

21. Each of the following agencies has authority to fix some price or rate EXCEPT the 21.___
    A. Board of Governors of the Federal Reserve System
    B. SEC
    C. ICC
    D. Public Service Commission

22. In the matter of appraising the value of public utilities for purposes of rate regulation, the Supreme Court has 22.___
    A. adopted the theory of prudent cost less depreciation
    B. favored the theory of reproduction cost
    C. given no clear-cut support to either doctrine
    D. ruled that each state may set up its own guides for its public service commissions

23. The risks due to speculative production tend to be increased by 23.___
    A. improved transportation
    B. improved market information
    C. monopoly
    D. the roundabout method of production

24. The equation $\frac{MV + M'V'}{T} = P$ 24.___
    A. was formulated to explain why wages lag behind prices
    B. is related to the quantity theory of money
    C. obviates the need for index numbers in measuring price changes
    D. was evolved by Adam Smith

25. Indicate by reference to the groupings below which of the following statements are TRUE about wages. 25.___
    I. Wages are determined in accordance with the same general principles which apply to all prices.
    II. An increase in the supply of capital tends to raise wages.
    III. The current level of wages is a determinant of the demand for labor.
    IV. Wage differentials result from the existence of non-competing groups.

The CORRECT answer is:
A. I, III
B. II, IV
C. I, III, IV
D. I, II, III, IV

KEY (CORRECT ANSWERS)

1. A	6. C	11. C	16. D	21. B
2. B	7. B	12. A	17. A	22. C
3. B	8. B	13. B	18. D	23. D
4. D	9. B	14. D	19. B	24. B
5. A	10. C	15. D	20. A	25. D

ANSWER SHEET

TEST NO. ________________ PART ________ TITLE OF POSITION ______________________________
(AS GIVEN IN EXAMINATION ANNOUNCEMENT - INCLUDE OPTION, IF ANY)

PLACE OF EXAMINATION ______________________________ ______________________________ DATE ________
(CITY OR TOWN) (STATE)

RATING

USE THE SPECIAL PENCIL. MAKE GLOSSY BLACK MARKS.

1	A B C D E	26	A B C D E	51	A B C D E	76	A B C D E	101	A B C D E
2	A B C D E	27	A B C D E	52	A B C D E	77	A B C D E	102	A B C D E
3	A B C D E	28	A B C D E	53	A B C D E	78	A B C D E	103	A B C D E
4	A B C D E	29	A B C D E	54	A B C D E	79	A B C D E	104	A B C D E
5	A B C D E	30	A B C D E	55	A B C D E	80	A B C D E	105	A B C D E
6	A B C D E	31	A B C D E	56	A B C D E	81	A B C D E	106	A B C D E
7	A B C D E	32	A B C D E	57	A B C D E	82	A B C D E	107	A B C D E
8	A B C D E	33	A B C D E	58	A B C D E	83	A B C D E	108	A B C D E
9	A B C D E	34	A B C D E	59	A B C D E	84	A B C D E	109	A B C D E
10	A B C D E	35	A B C D E	60	A B C D E	85	A B C D E	110	A B C D E

Make only ONE mark for each answer. Additional and stray marks may be counted as mistakes. In making corrections, erase errors COMPLETELY.

11	A B C D E	36	A B C D E	61	A B C D E	86	A B C D E	111	A B C D E
12	A B C D E	37	A B C D E	62	A B C D E	87	A B C D E	112	A B C D E
13	A B C D E	38	A B C D E	63	A B C D E	88	A B C D E	113	A B C D E
14	A B C D E	39	A B C D E	64	A B C D E	89	A B C D E	114	A B C D E
15	A B C D E	40	A B C D E	65	A B C D E	90	A B C D E	115	A B C D E
16	A B C D E	41	A B C D E	66	A B C D E	91	A B C D E	116	A B C D E
17	A B C D E	42	A B C D E	67	A B C D E	92	A B C D E	117	A B C D E
18	A B C D E	43	A B C D E	68	A B C D E	93	A B C D E	118	A B C D E
19	A B C D E	44	A B C D E	69	A B C D E	94	A B C D E	119	A B C D E
20	A B C D E	45	A B C D E	70	A B C D E	95	A B C D E	120	A B C D E
21	A B C D E	46	A B C D E	71	A B C D E	96	A B C D E	121	A B C D E
22	A B C D E	47	A B C D E	72	A B C D E	97	A B C D E	122	A B C D E
23	A B C D E	48	A B C D E	73	A B C D E	98	A B C D E	123	A B C D E
24	A B C D E	49	A B C D E	74	A B C D E	99	A B C D E	124	A B C D E
25	A B C D E	50	A B C D E	75	A B C D E	100	A B C D E	125	A B C D E

ANSWER SHEET

TEST NO. ____________ PART ________ TITLE OF POSITION ____________________________
(AS GIVEN IN EXAMINATION ANNOUNCEMENT - INCLUDE OPTION, IF ANY)

PLACE OF EXAMINATION ____________________________ ____________________ DATE ____________
(CITY OR TOWN) (STATE)

RATING

USE THE SPECIAL PENCIL. MAKE GLOSSY BLACK MARKS.

1 A B C D E	26 A B C D E	51 A B C D E	76 A B C D E	101 A B C D E
2 A B C D E	27 A B C D E	52 A B C D E	77 A B C D E	102 A B C D E
3 A B C D E	28 A B C D E	53 A B C D E	78 A B C D E	103 A B C D E
4 A B C D E	29 A B C D E	54 A B C D E	79 A B C D E	104 A B C D E
5 A B C D E	30 A B C D E	55 A B C D E	80 A B C D E	105 A B C D E
6 A B C D E	31 A B C D E	56 A B C D E	81 A B C D E	106 A B C D E
7 A B C D E	32 A B C D E	57 A B C D E	82 A B C D E	107 A B C D E
8 A B C D E	33 A B C D E	58 A B C D E	83 A B C D E	108 A B C D E
9 A B C D E	34 A B C D E	59 A B C D E	84 A B C D E	109 A B C D E
10 A B C D E	35 A B C D E	60 A B C D E	85 A B C D E	110 A B C D E

Make only ONE mark for each answer. Additional and stray marks may be counted as mistakes. In making corrections, erase errors COMPLETELY.

11 A B C D E	36 A B C D E	61 A B C D E	86 A B C D E	111 A B C D E
12 A B C D E	37 A B C D E	62 A B C D E	87 A B C D E	112 A B C D E
13 A B C D E	38 A B C D E	63 A B C D E	88 A B C D E	113 A B C D E
14 A B C D E	39 A B C D E	64 A B C D E	89 A B C D E	114 A B C D E
15 A B C D E	40 A B C D E	65 A B C D E	90 A B C D E	115 A B C D E
16 A B C D E	41 A B C D E	66 A B C D E	91 A B C D E	116 A B C D E
17 A B C D E	42 A B C D E	67 A B C D E	92 A B C D E	117 A B C D E
18 A B C D E	43 A B C D E	68 A B C D E	93 A B C D E	118 A B C D E
19 A B C D E	44 A B C D E	69 A B C D E	94 A B C D E	119 A B C D E
20 A B C D E	45 A B C D E	70 A B C D E	95 A B C D E	120 A B C D E
21 A B C D E	46 A B C D E	71 A B C D E	96 A B C D E	121 A B C D E
22 A B C D E	47 A B C D E	72 A B C D E	97 A B C D E	122 A B C D E
23 A B C D E	48 A B C D E	73 A B C D E	98 A B C D E	123 A B C D E
24 A B C D E	49 A B C D E	74 A B C D E	99 A B C D E	124 A B C D E
25 A B C D E	50 A B C D E	75 A B C D E	100 A B C D E	125 A B C D E